The Essentials of Managing Risk for Projects and Programmes

The Essentials of Managing Risk for Projects and Programmes is an indispensable, practical guide to the steps that lead to success in managing risk.

Risk management is particularly important for projects and programmes, since they all carry varying degrees of risk. The combination of uniqueness, constraints, assumptions, stakeholder expectations, changing environment and human behaviour all conspire to make projects and programmes risky ventures. Rather than presenting new theories or techniques or tools, John Bartlett offers down-to-earth guidelines and proven methods to respond to risk appropriately.

Pick up and use this concise, intensely practical guide to develop a shared understanding, shared language and shared purpose across project managers, programme managers, sponsors, risk managers, project and programme board members and associated stakeholders in all your projects and programmes.

John Bartlett is an author with a deep business experience of directing change through projects and programmes. He is a Fellow of the Association for Project Management and has written widely on the subject, including three books on risk management, programme management and quality management.

The Essentials of Project and Programme Management

Over the last fifteen years projects and programmes have become part of the everyday activities of organizations large and small. Understanding the essentials of how to plan projects, manage programmes or handle risk represents knowledge and skills that have moved beyond the purview of specialist project managers into the world of the generalists. Books in The Essentials of Project and Programme Management series are written for project sponsors, project team members, project owners, new project managers and others who work on the periphery of projects or are drawn into project teams on a temporary basis. The series is characterised by very readable, concise and applied books that provide an essential grounding in the context, skills and behaviours associated with successful project working.

The Essentials of Project Management 4e
Dennis Lock

The Essentials of Managing Programmes 6e
John Bartlett

The Essentials of Managing Risk for Projects and Programmes 3e
John Bartlett

The Essentials of Managing Quality for Projects and Programmes 2e
John Bartlett

The Essentials of Managing Risk for Projects and Programmes

Third edition

John Bartlett

Routledge
Taylor & Francis Group

LONDON AND NEW YORK

Third edition published 2017
by Routledge
2 Park Square, Milton Park, Abingdon, Oxon, OX14 4RN

and by Routledge
711 Third Avenue, New York, NY 10017

Routledge is an imprint of the Taylor & Francis Group, an informa business

© 2017 John Bartlett

Second edition published by Project Manager Today Publications, 2008.

British Library Cataloguing-in-Publication Data
A catalogue record for this book is available from the British Library

Library of Congress Cataloguing-in-Publication Data
A catalog record for this book has been requested

ISBN: 978-1-138-28830-0 (hbk)
ISBN: 978-1-138-28831-7 (pbk)
ISBN: 978-1-315-26799-9 (ebk)

Typeset in Bembo
by Apex CoVantage, LLC

Contents

Illustrations

Figures

Tables

Foreword

The word "risk" has entered the public consciousness in a new way recently, following terrorist outrages, public health scares and outbreaks of infectious animal diseases. We hear the term from politicians, businessmen, newscasters, social workers, military advisers, journalists, doctors – everywhere people seem to be highlighting the risks we face in all aspects of life. But it appears that less is being said about "risk management", the process by which we can understand the risks to which we are exposed, and then act appropriately.

Risk management is particularly important for projects and programmes, since they are specifically designed to take risks. The combination of uniqueness, constraints, assumptions, stakeholder expectations, changing environment, and human behaviour all conspire to make projects and programmes risky ventures. As a result, those of us involved with projects and programmes must inevitably come to terms with how to make risk management work if we are to stand any chance of meeting our objectives. If anyone should know about risk and its management, it should be project and programme managers and their teams.

And yet the field of project and programme management is littered with failures, as unforeseen events and circumstances strike home with depressing regularity. Surely we can do better than this? Is "unforeseen" the same as "unforeseeable"? Are we doomed to repeat the failures of the past indefinitely? Can risk management ever be effective, making a positive contribution to achievement of objectives, focussing attention on key areas requiring management attention, and maximising the chances of project and programme success?

It is at this point that John Bartlett's book should make a difference. We don't need new theories or techniques or tools in order to make risk management effective. Instead we need practical guidelines on how to make it work. Drawing on his wide experience as a project and programme manager, John offers advice from the battlefield. His "view from the trenches" will help others to know what to expect before they go over the top, and will prepare them for what lies ahead. This book will be valuable for the hard-pressed project or programme manager who knows that he or she is at risk, and wants to know what to do about it.

Often too much effort is spent on risk identification and analysis, leaving managers like rabbits caught in the headlights, seeing what is coming towards them but seemingly unable to react. The message of this book is a call to risk management, offering practical and proven methods to respond to risk appropriately and effectively. Putting the contents into practice will certainly help to manage risks on projects and programmes, and hopefully start to reverse the tide of failure which has become all too familiar. Paraphrasing Einstein, if you always do what you've always done, you'll always get what you always got. It is possible to do things differently and deal proactively with project and programme risk – this book shows you how.

Dr. David Hillson, HonFAPM, PMI Fellow,
FIRM, CMgr, FCMI
The Risk Doctor, The Risk Doctor Partnership

Preface to the Third Edition

In my frequent role as a project auditor I have seen many interpretations of risk management – some of these have been good and some have been poor. In many cases, project teams seem to be inventing and re-inventing risk management processes, such that there is little consistency or continuity of practice. Project management methodologies all extol the virtues of good risk management but rarely show how it should be tackled in practice. This often leaves project teams very much in the dark when it comes to applying risk management for positive effect.

My current view is that, on the whole, risk management is still being tackled badly in many projects and often ranked below other project elements in importance, such as the project schedule, resource plan and status reporting. Small wonder then that we continually hear of projects failing.

What I'm finding is a series of inconsistent practices in the name of risk management, many of which are ineffectual in actually reducing risk. I find that many project managers can become stuck in a *High, Medium, Low* mentality in terms of assessing risk, or are expressing risks using only one or two words. I also find that much time is spent recording risks but little time spent in showing real progress in risk mitigation. Actions to reduce risk are often absent or not given appropriate attention.

It is almost as if some project teams are paying lip service to the universally recognised view that risk management should be undertaken on projects, without understanding the true value of doing so. Yet, risk management practised well should be able to reduce significantly the chances of cost overruns, gross margin erosion, scope creep and a host of other typical project impacts. There are enlightened project teams who recognise this and whilst they may be in short supply they have regularly shown how risk management can contribute to the achievement of a successful project.

A big problem is that project managers are often poor risk managers. The two roles require quite different mindsets. The single minded task manager is quite different from the lateral thinking risk identifier. Yet project management methodologies expect the project manager to manage project risk; so why should we be surprised when risk management is not given the attention it deserves?

This book attempts to address the widespread poor attention given to risk in projects and programmes. It aims to provide the reader with a sufficient understanding of the subject in order to practise consistently good risk management. It also shows why risk management should be the premier focus for project managers, over and above the other project management elements. It is not a book about the history of risk or the science of probability. It is rather a book that gives a practical view of risk management for any type of project or programme.

John Bartlett, BA Hons (Lond), FRGS, FRSA,
Hon.FAPM, CPM, LTCL, ALCM, LLCM

Acknowledgements

I am especially grateful to Dr. David Hillson, Director of The Risk Doctor Partnership for writing the Foreword to this book. Also, to Richard Watson, BSc(Eng), CEng, MICE, for sharing his valuable experience in engineering risk management.

I acknowledge the support of NCR Ltd. for allowing me to share information regarding their highly successful implementation of the Euro programme.

About the author

After a long career in project management and consulting for a varied public and private client set whilst employed at IBM UK Ltd., John Bartlett became Head of Project Management for the UK and Ireland at DMR Consulting Group in the late 1990s. Latterly, he was Director of UK Technology Services and a Director of the European Programme Office at NCR Ltd. From 2004, he concentrated on PM consultancy and teaching, acting as an independent consultant. In retirement he continues to maintain thought leadership in his fields and is active with several PM-related organisations.

In his career, John has managed and directed several large-scale projects and programmes, including the *Implementation of the Euro* for NCR, where an extended workforce and multiple stakeholders across twelve countries required novel risk management techniques. At IBM he was engaged in programme and project management on behalf of clients in various business sectors, including government, insurance, banking and finance, retail, automotive and engineering. He was involved in the management of IBM's Year 2000 Programme in Europe, and formed part of the Programme Executive team.

He is an Honorary Fellow of the UK Association for Project Management and an APM Certified Project Manager. He has published many papers in project management subjects and several books, which include: *Managing Programmes of Business Change*; *The Essentials of Managing Risks for Projects and Programmes*; and *Right First and Every Time – Managing Quality in Projects and Programmes*. He also has a strong interest in music and the arts, and has published numerous music compositions and reference books on decorative ceramics.

1   Introduction

Thinking about risk

There is risk in everything we do. Crossing a busy road, bungee jumping, white-water rafting, making an investment decision and building a house are actions and activities which all contain risk. A participant in any of these is likely to weigh up the risks before taking part.

The nature of the risk assessment, of course, will vary greatly and will depend on the activity and the value the participant places on it with respect to personal risk. For example, crossing a busy road might be perceived by a young, streetwise city dweller to be such a mundane action that it requires only a cursory, almost subconscious thought before embarking on it. To an elderly country dweller, however, the same action might merit considerably greater thought. Yet, whereas it is possible to make such generalised statements regarding these two stereotypes, it is by no means certain that they will apply in every occurrence. Extenuating circumstances could cause the elderly country dweller to make no assessment of risk before crossing the road and vice versa.

What is more certain, though, is that none of these stereotypes is likely to undertake a *written* risk assessment before carrying out the action. Undertaking a written assessment is more likely in activities such as making an investment decision or building a house, but again, it depends on how risk averse the participant is. Our perception is that few of our daily actions merit a formal risk management approach. We tend to balance monetary value against time and personal safety in arriving at the degree of risk we should take.

We are likely to identify with the newspaper headline *"Elderly man injured crossing road"* in terms of how the accident could have occurred, since we tend to take a view that elderly people are more vulnerable in this situation. The headline *"City student injured crossing road"* might cause us to search harder for causes, since we instinctively expect this situation to be a rarer event.

The moral here is that generalisation is fine as a starting point, though it rarely yields the best risk assessment. We need to apply greater depth to thinking about risk, but this does not mean it has to be a laboured activity.

Talking about risk to a colleague from the Far East recently, I was intrigued to discover that the Chinese word for "risk" is appropriately "wēi jī", meaning "danger opportunity".

危
机

The juxtaposition of both the positive and negative aspects of risk seemed to me to make perfect sense. However, many projects tend to focus only on the negative aspect, whereas the business case for bothering with risk at all must surely focus on the positive aspect. I am convinced that good risk management is the key to many of the ills about which contemporary projects complain: cost overruns, schedule conflicts, scope creep and resource shortages.

A question I like to ask project managers is *"How often do you spend time on risk management in your projects?"*. The answer is rarely *"once a week"*, never *"daily"*, sometimes *"once a month"* and often *"once a quarter"*. The answer varies, though, according to the type of project. For IT-related and general business projects, the above is usually the norm. For safety critical engineering projects, I would hope that the answer would be different and that more attention would be given to risk management. Even so, I often hear that risk management is deficient in many examples of safety critical projects.

It is possible, of course, to manage a project without any form of risk management, but this itself carries a degree of risk. There will always be situations that could have been handled more efficiently or cost effectively had risk management techniques been employed. Don't forget the dual nature of risk where opportunity is just as appropriate as danger. Risk management is often a trade-off between that which is essential to be achieved and that which is not. In other words, how assured do you want to be of a project's outcome?

My view is that a project manager should be thinking about risk on a daily basis – not necessarily formally, but at least informally. If weekly status reports are not showing differences in the risk register then insufficient attention is being given to risk management. The old saying amongst project managers *"How do projects become late?"* answered by *"One day at a time"* has a worrying ring of truth. It is often the incremental "creep" of projects in terms of scope, timescale and earned value that give credence to this saying. The only way we can tackle this problem is by practising risk management techniques, and on a daily basis. It does not mean that the project manager should be constructing risk analysis charts every day. It means that he or she should be applying thought in a risk-oriented way, and developing "risk-thinking teams" – but more of this later.

Some attempt to simplify what is, in fact, a complex subject, is sometimes made by prescribing templates. Indeed, I have often been asked for a "starter set of risks" for a particular type of project, as if all conform to a level of predictability. The very notion that risk management is an exact science and so is able to be prescribed by templates is a much-held fallacy.

The danger of prescription is that it can lead the project manager into a false sense of security – i.e., for very little effort the project manager can feel he or she has produced a viable risk plan. Risk management does require particular effort, however, and should not be dismissed as a trivial exercise. Prescription can also stifle creativity, preventing project managers from giving deep thought to the real risks in a project. Templates can only test generalised and historically identified risks. They cannot test the specific combinations of objectives and activities that will be unique to the project. Good risk management is not prescriptive, but it should, of course, be able to draw on previous experience. There will be plenty of projects where a checklist of previous experience is a particularly useful starting point.

The risk–issue–change pathway

I find project managers are almost universally good at knowing that when an issue has occurred something has to be done to resolve it. They may not know *what* has to be done, but they certainly know that a process needs to be invoked. The issue is recorded and reported at Progress Meetings, where it is then probably discussed. Such issues, or *problems* as some prefer to call them, will demand time and, therefore, cost expenditure in order to resolve them. If a project change has to be raised in order to resolve an issue then this could bring an even greater cost. Also, there are often further risks associated with making a change and resolving an issue. Figure 1.1 illustrates this.

Figure 1.1 The link between risks, issues, changes and the relative cost of dealing with each

When a project is completed, the project close-out meeting invariably debates the issues that occurred during the life of the project. How much more efficient it might have been if many of the issues could have been foreseen as risks, and tackled as such! The cost of impact could have been saved. The "fire-fighting" and running around trying to solve something urgently could have been avoided. There would have been no unplanned disruption to tasks, and the possibility of follow-on risks through resolving the issues could also have been avoided.

Surprisingly, though, few people make the connection between risks and issues. Today's risks are tomorrow's issues. Yet, if it is more efficient to deal with risks than issues, why do so few people think along these lines?

I believe it is partly a difficulty in differentiating between risks and issues (the next chapter explores this) and partly a lack of precision that causes people to ignore the risks. It is easy to identify an issue, because it is here and present. A risk may impact at any time in the future – *who can be precise about that?* It is a difficult business case to persuade management to release money and resources to tackle a risk on such an expectation.

Yet experience shows that those who *are* able to "bet the project" and spend money tackling risks benefit significantly.

Many projects set aside an amount for risk in the original project business case. This might be a standard percentage or, infrequently, a figure derived from calculating an initial risk exposure. I find it strange, though, that having set aside this amount, managers are often reluctant to spend it on identifying and tackling risks. It is as if the money set aside in the name of risk is really for resolving issues, i.e., when risks impact. This reverse logic is symptomatic of a focus on issues and a lack of risk-thinking, which many project teams display.

Risks, issues and changes are often termed project *exceptions*, in that they are exceptional events (or ought to be) during a project's lifespan. As project exceptions they have one thing in common – *actions*. Each needs one or more actions to tackle it. It is useful to know this since, as actions occur elsewhere in the cycle of project control, it is possible to be consistent about their presentation. Thus, actions from a project progress meeting can be recorded in a similar way to actions from project exceptions. Ideally, actions should appear as tasks on the project plan, since the performance of actions requires time and effort, as does any other project activity. This provides a valuable management link between the plan and project exceptions. These latter should not be thought of as separate entities, though many tend to manage them as such. (More on managing actions may be found in Chapter 4, *Responding to risk*.)

Understanding the risk-issue-change pathway is vital for developing a risk-thinking attitude. Occasionally, though, this can be abused. It is easy to fill a risk register with risks and pay lip service to a process, so that when an impact occurs, a claim could be made that it was not the project manager's fault because the risk was recorded and reported. A true risk-thinking attitude is about taking mental ownership of the risks and an active desire to ensure that they don't impact as issues. This can be measured, of course, though I have yet to see a

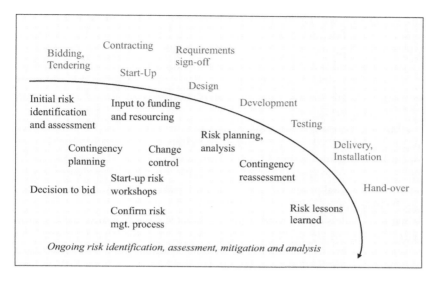

Figure 1.2 Typical risk management activities in relation to project phases

contract specify "no more than ten risks should impact as issues"! What *is* specified is the bottom line. Project managers are frequently measured against budget, time and quality, and good risk management has the ability to influence these outcomes significantly.

Risk management applicability

When and where to apply risk management is a question frequently asked. If you accept my view that it should be thought about at least daily, then the identification and assessment of risk is an ongoing activity right across a project or programme's lifespan. There are, however, specific points in a lifespan where risk management is particularly relevant. Figure 1.2 shows some typical risk management activities across project phases.

Pre-contract stage

Risk management plays an essential role well before a project gets underway. At the bidding or tendering stage it is important to identify and assess risks before proceeding to contract. The allocation of funding and resources should always be based on a formal risk assessment. Companies tend to have different ways of doing this, depending on their business requirements. Some use software questionnaires that produce weighted assessments of risk according to how questions are answered. Others open formal risk registers at this stage, so that risks identified can be seamlessly transferred into project execution.

Less widespread is any formal calculation of risk reserves for contingencies. Many companies will decide on a percentage of the total project cost for risk, e.g., 5% or 10%. For very little effort, however, it is possible to calculate a proper risk exposure. The margin of error will be much less than any "finger in the air" guesswork and both the project team and the financiers will gain a degree of assurance through knowing that it is calculated from gathered data rather than guesswork. (Details of risk exposure calculation may be found in Chapter 6, *Analysing and reporting risk.*)

Establishing contingencies and contingency reserves at the pre-contract stage is important because they have a significant effect on project funding. I suspect most businesses would rather know at this stage not only the cost of a project in terms of resources over time but also its risk exposure. The former plus the latter equals the total potential cost of the undertaking. Any subsequent changes might be extra, of course.

What is often less understood at pre-contract stage is that any risk assessment undertaken will firstly yield unmitigated risks, i.e., risks that represent a risk exposure without any consideration of mitigating actions. The specification of actions to respond to identified risks should bring down the risk exposure considerably, assuming the actions are carried out successfully. This mitigated risk exposure is effectively a bet on good risk management. If the level of risk can be managed down then the amount of reserve required for risks can be significantly reduced. It is important, therefore, to state whether assessed risks are unmitigated or mitigated when discussing the potential cost of a project with a client. Merely going to a sponsor or client with a figure of £3m needed for risk is insufficient. With mitigating actions that figure might be reduced to £0.8m.

Project start-up

Essential activities at project start-up are the establishment of a formal risk management process, to which all parties agree to subscribe, plus a start-up risk workshop. This latter activity rechecks the validity of the risks transferred from the pre-contract stage. Since all interested parties should be present (core team, suppliers, customers/users, etc.), it is a good opportunity to get the team into a risk-thinking frame of mind at an early phase of the project. (See Chapter 2, *Identifying and expressing risk,* for information about running a Risk Identification Workshop.)

Once the project requirements have been formally signed off, the project should be under change control. Risk management has an important role to play during change control. Any project change being proposed should be assessed for risks. In fact, no change should be approved unless the impact of the change has been risk assessed. This should include revisiting the current project risk register, in case the application of the change may alter probabilities, impacts and the validity and cost of actions and contingency plans.

Table 1.1 Sample of tolerances

Consideration	Tolerance
Scope	zero tolerance
Quality	zero tolerance
Time	+ 1 week
Cost	+ 10% maximum, without further authorisation

As a project gets underway, risk planning and analysis need to become ongoing activities. The assignment of actions to contain risk and the monitoring of their progress and effectiveness is a fundamental part of risk planning. (Chapter 4, *Responding to risk*, explores this activity in detail.)

The parallel activity of risk analysis is an important contributor to project decision-making, and something which many projects fail to undertake correctly. The project manager and sponsors need to be assured that the risk of moving forward is acceptable in terms of aspects such as cost, timescale and quality. (Refer to Chapter 6, *Analysing and reporting risk,* for details of this important activity.)

Tolerances may be defined to allow the project manager leeway in the management of risk. These are typically aligned to cost, time and quality. Table 1.1 shows an example.

Project execution

The development phase of a project often presents a polarised view of risk. It can, on the one hand, reassure project teams that the risks identified at project start-up are not so risky after all, or, on the other hand, reveal more risk if the deliverables being constructed are not as easy as originally believed. Of course, much depends on the nature of the project in this respect. Software development projects can be particularly problematic. Those using Agile or RAD techniques (rapid application development), where phases are compressed, tend to reveal more risk during component construction. R&D (research and development) projects often commence with a high-risk perspective, owing to the unfamiliarity of the work to be undertaken, and then reveal less risk as the project progresses and the team becomes more familiar with the product under development.

As a project moves into its testing phase it is worth reassessing the contingencies already identified for those risks whose impacts could have damaging consequences. Testing can reveal new information about a deliverable that can change the perspective of any associated risks. It can also generate new risks. It is, therefore, a good opportunity to revisit the risk exposures of risks with contingencies. Testing may reveal that some contingencies will not be required (therefore, less cost) or that some contingencies may need to be increased (therefore, more cost).

Project completion

At project completion it is important to analyse the risks that were encountered and debate whether these were handled in the most appropriate and efficient way. Information learned from this activity can be used on future projects. When looking at lessons learned during a Project Completion Review, for example, some teams analyse only the issues encountered in the project. Few ask whether these issues could have been foreseen as risks. Yet merely examining this aspect can significantly help combat scope creep and margin erosion in future projects.

The programme view

At a programme level, risk management additionally includes the risk of benefits achievement. Otherwise, risk management plays a role similar to projects across a programme's phases:

*   During *Programme Feasibility* it confirms the viability of the programme and provides the basis for judgements concerning the required investment and expected benefits.
*   During *Programme Design* it supports the establishment of a firm foundation, building the confidence and assurance required to get the programme off to a good start.
*   During *Programme Execution* it provides a sound basis for ongoing management of the total programme risk exposure, and supports the requirements for problem resolution and programme changes.
*   During *Benefits Realisation* it supports the successful transfer to the business of completed projects, the achievement of projected benefits and performance levels, the redeployment of resources and the feedback of "lessons learned".

A programme also has the benefits of scale, in that risk data can be rolled up from its constituent projects. Thus, risks identified in one project might also be applicable to another, so the programme risk manager is able to develop mitigation strategies suitable to both. Savings may be made in this way, and the economy of scale can be a significant benefit from taking a programme view of risk.

For more information on managing risks in programmes, see my other book in this series, entitled *The Essentials of Managing Programmes.*

The business case for practising risk management

Managing risk takes time and costs money. *Is it really worth doing on every project?* Hindsight invariably shows that it *is* worth doing. Quite apart from the side effects of confidence building and team building that risk management can bring, the benefit to the bottom line is usually significant.

If you take the case of potential margin erosion, caused by things such as scope creep and rework, risk management can reduce or even prevent it. Too many projects overrun their costs. The amount of overrun or a good proportion of it could have been a calculated risk exposure at project outset, and this risk exposure could have been mitigated.

As an example, take a project with a budget of £50,000 that comes in at £75,000. If good risk management had been applied, the £25,000 overrun could have been identified as an initial risk exposure. Mitigation could have reduced this significantly. The £25,000 overrun need never have occurred.

I always cringe when I read about the massive overruns that some projects generate. *Was a risk exposure ever calculated? If so, were the risks mitigated? Surely, no one should embark on a project costing more than £100,000 without doing so?*

Risk management is also a state of mind. A risk-thinking team brings benefits not only to a project but to the business as a whole. Such a team is confident, assured and will apply a creativity to work that might not otherwise develop. Risk management demands creativity in effecting the resolutions to potentially difficult problems. Avoidance, workarounds and contingencies need creative planning. These skills can be transferred to the normal business operation.

This brings into focus the importance of an organisation's culture to the practice of risk management. A risk-thinking team does not happen overnight but develops as an organisation becomes more mature in risk management. There have been several attempts at defining maturity levels for risk management. There is currently no national standard, but it is not difficult to establish a company-specific table of risk maturity, which can act as a roadmap to achieving the cultural and process changes needed for risk management excellence.

I have helped several organisations in various industries accomplish such a roadmap. Table 1.1 shows a summary of my own checklist for risk maturity. The first step is for an organisation to decide where they might be currently on the scale. This might be relatively easy to state or it might require a short period of study of all risk practices throughout the organisation. There can be significant revelations in undertaking a study. For example, I have known a construction company's engineering department practising around Level 4, completely in isolation to the rest of the company which is at Level 0 or 0.5.

A roadmap based on risk maturity levels enables a company or organisation to decide to what level it would like to operate. Significant sponsorship and investment is needed to attain the higher levels, but the rewards can well surpass the investment. Walking in to a Level 5 operating organisation reveals immediately behaviours that are unusual in most office environments. There is, for example, strong evidence of proactive working, information sharing, confident and fast decision-making and risk taking. This exalted level is rare, but increasingly companies are seeing the need to develop beyond their current lower level, as business efficiency and due diligence are becoming a corporate necessity. Level 3

Level	Description	Practice	Indications
Level 0	Ad Hoc RM	Inconsistent, isolated use of some RM techniques.	Operations largely reactive; frequent fire-fighting.
Level 1	Risk Register Usage	Risk Identification, Qualified Evaluation and Responses.	Local sponsorship of RM and some acceptance of benefits.
Level 2	Risk Quantification	Percentage Probabilities, monetary values for Impacts; Risk Exposure calculation.	Corporate sponsorship of RM; widespread acceptance of benefits.
Level 3	Risk Modelling	Risk interdependencies; Worst-Case Scenarios; Horizon Scanning; Monte Carlo Simulation. Company sponsored RM processes.	Operations largely proactive; risk responses funded and supported; visible decrease in issues. Less risk aversion – more risk taking.
Level 4	Risk Opportunities	Calculation of Expected Values. Teams look to turn threats into opportunities. "Reuse" practised. Analysis of trends.	Solid issue prevention and lessons learned cultures evident. Widespread risk taking. Opportunity seeking.
Level 5	Risk Performance	Budgetary provisions for mitigated risk; Risk KPIs for managers and project managers.	A risk-thinking culture dominant. Visible benefits to the bottom line

*KPI = Key Performance Indicator

Figure 1.3 My own Risk Maturity Table

is readily attainable for most organisations and there are real business benefits as a result. Just decreasing the fire-fighting can have a noticeable effect on productivity, for example.

There is no doubt that risk management underwrites decision-making. Being able to gather data and assess the risk of making a decision is fundamental to business. The more mature an organisation is in risk management the better its decision-making.

Feel free to use or adapt my Risk Maturity Table (Figure 1.3) for your own purposes, but if you publish it internally, please acknowledge its source.

2 Identifying and expressing risk

This is the bit project managers and project teams generally do not like doing! They know it has to be done, but it is often seen as a chore. This is probably why risk is sometimes only identified once during a project – at project outset, when all the team comes together for the first time. The challenge is: *How do we make risk identification and assessment interesting, important, and something that is practised at least weekly and thought about on a daily basis?*

Getting people to think about risk is, for many project teams, a cultural shift. Few project teams have been taught formally how to develop *risk-thinking* approaches. There are many courses that teach the basics of risk management as a process, but few that concentrate on thought processes for good risk management. In the introduction to this book I mention that we often subconsciously weigh up risks, such as when crossing the road. Businesses frequently require a more overt practice and many companies have dreamed up various ways to tackle this. Ubiquitous amongst these is the *risk checklist* – a way of formalising a judgmental process.

The risk checklist exists in many forms and attempts to give some assurance to the identification of risk. A series of questions or situations are typically presented, to which the project manager is required to respond. Responses are then weighted and an overall risk score is given. Depending on the score threshold the rating is usually low, medium or high risk. Anything above low risk may trigger a specialist review or sign-off.

Whilst this formalisation gets people to participate in a risk process, it is very mechanical, and such prescribed processes usually leave no room for creativity. Risk questions or situations are good for setting the scene and can be thought-provoking. However, as most projects are unique, there needs to be room to respond to the uniqueness of the project and the freedom to consider novel approaches to managing its risk.

The risk checklist is particularly useful for repeated operations, such as for a bidding process. I've seen sales forces use a checklist to answer questions about their proposals. These are scored and sent to a regional or divisional sign-off for approval. Over time in a repeated operation, the questions can be refined so that it becomes less likely for a risk not to be considered up front. Of course, even though a completed checklist may give a low (i.e., risky) score, management could still make a decision to run with the risk. At least in this case, the checklist can serve as an audit trail.

A key starting point in tackling the attitudes to risk is to ensure that everyone knows how to identify and express risk in a foolproof way. Quite apart from promoting consistency, this enables everyone to overcome any fear factors in addressing risk and to ensure that the differences between a risk and an issue are fully understood.

Expressing risk

Many project teams seem to have a major difficulty in expressing risk, i.e., articulating the risk so that others can fully comprehend it. There is also widespread ignorance of the differences between a risk and an issue, such that many risks are often really issues and vice versa. If risks and issues are expressed correctly, however, there should be no doubt which is which.

Let's tackle the expression of risk first and then look at the differences between risks and issues.

In my role as auditor, I have often been presented with risk registers that look like this:

Risk	Probability	Impact	Mitigation
Pipe-flow testing	H	M	Check schedule.
Testing resources	M	H	Assess resource requirement.

This, I'm afraid, is often the norm for many projects. It is symptomatic of someone who has realised that risks need to be identified and logged and is paying lip service to a procedural requirement. The question is: *"Where's the risk?"* It's a good question to ask, since what I have shown above are merely statements of project elements. They might be areas in which risks may reside, but they are not risks in themselves and they are not fully expressed risk statements. In fact, they are quite good categories for risk investigation, but more of that later.

Responses we might get to our question are:

1. *Pipe-flow testing may be late.*
2. *We may not have enough resources for pipe-flow testing.*

That's better, the statements are looking more like risks, but we are missing some vital information. What's causing the risks?

Let's take the first risk. A typical response might be:

1. *Because of a need to add extra routing to the design, there is a risk that pipe-flow testing may be late.*

Much better. But what's the effect?

Well, the project might overrun.

OK, so the risk is better expressed as:

1. *Because of a need to add extra routing to the design, there is a risk that planned pipe-flow testing may be late, resulting in a delay to the project schedule.*

Perfect. Now we have cause, risk and effect, and in one sentence! Little risk of ambiguity now!

Because of a need to add extra routing to the design	*there is a risk that planned pipe-flow testing may be late*	*resulting in a delay to the project schedule.*
Cause	Risk	Effect

The risk has been properly expressed as a risk statement, embodying the essential elements of cause, event and impact.

What about the other risk? How about:

2. *Because of the holiday period, there is a risk that insufficient resources will be available for pipe-flow testing, resulting in an extended testing period.*

Also much better!

For the risk register to have any value, though, we need to record more than just the statement of risk. A few control factors would be useful. Chapter 5, *Recording risk*, shows how to record a risk, once identified.

Take care when crafting causes. If a cause could also be written as a risk then it is possible that the true underlying cause has not been identified. For example, consider the following risk statement:

> *Because there might be a transport strike, there is a risk that staff may not be able to get to the planned training sessions, resulting in delay to the project completion.*

The cause might also be expressed as the central risk: *There is a risk of a transport strike, resulting in staff not being able to get to training sessions, thus delaying the project completion.* This tells us that the transport strike is not the true cause. The clue to the faulty cause lies in the words "because there *might be*". In other words, the cause is not specific enough. We need to search for the true cause of the transport strike. So, the following risk statement is better:

> *Because of discontent in the transportation workforce, there is a risk of a transport strike, resulting in staff not being able to get to training sessions, thus delaying the project completion.*

The discontent in the transportation workforce is a stated fact, so it represents the cause better. Of course, you could go back further and try to find the root cause of the discontent!

Differences between risks and issues

Simplistically, an issue is a situation or an event that has occurred that will cause a detrimental impact to the project. Conversely, a risk is an event that has not yet occurred but may or may not occur in the future. The key question to ask is: "*Has the situation or event occurred, or not?*"

However, like most things connected with projects, there are some grey areas. These usually concern project situations, rather than events. For example, a situation may exist that deals with an event that has not yet happened but is expected to happen at a point in the future. A common example is "*Stage 1 requirements have not been signed off by the client*". This sort of statement is often cited as an issue, but it is actually closer to one or more risks. The requirements have to be signed off before the project can continue into its design phase. Currently they have not been signed off, but they are expected to be signed off in the near future.

Client requirements sign-off ought to be a task on the project plan. It is only if the sign-off is already late or there is some concern about the sign-off that it becomes a worry to the project manager. If the task is late, you may wonder whether it would be more appropriate to raise it as an issue. The question to ask is: "*Is the project immediately impacted?*" If the answer is "yes", then it is an issue. If the answer is "no", then it is a risk.

This situation could give rise to several risks, and could easily form part of the cause section of risk statements. Table 2.1 gives an example.

If, as predicted by the penultimate item in the above list, the client decides not to sign off the requirements, the decision point (or event) is clearly an issue. Something has to be done about it immediately. The project might be saved by agreeing to a rescope or it may have to be cancelled altogether.

Table 2.1 Different risks from similar causes

Cause	Risk	Effect
Because Stage 1 requirements have not been signed off by the client, owing to unavailability of key board members	*there is a risk that the design phase will be held up*	*resulting in a delay to the overall project schedule.*
Because Stage 1 requirements have not been signed off by the client, owing to general indecision in the business	*there is a risk of several scope changes during the design and development phases*	*resulting in a change to the project target end date and a significant increase in costs.*
Because Stage 1 requirements have not been signed off by the client, owing to a restructure of his business	*there is a risk that they may never be signed off*	*resulting in cancellation of the current project.*
Because Stage 1 requirements have not been signed off by the client in the current budgetary period	*there is a risk that the project will enter the next budgetary period*	*resulting in a delay to the release of vital development funds.*

There are many situations in projects where critical tasks are late, such as where a sub-contractor should have delivered something and it has not arrived. It is tempting to call these issues, but, as we have seen above, they are more often risks. However, if work is prevented from continuing without whatever should have been delivered, the lateness is clearly an issue.

It is important that each project understands when a situation or event should be raised as an issue or risk. If the chosen project management methodology does not specify this, then the Project Office or project manager should ensure that the project exceptions procedure does. There *will* be grey areas, but it is hoped that the above examples will give some valuable guidance.

Identifying risk

How do you identify risk? What is the best way of going about it?

Knowing how to express risk is a fundamental prelude to identifying it. The *cause* part of the risk statements we have examined points to a risk's origin. Risks will occur because of an event or situation. Therefore, we need to focus firstly on the things that can cause risk. These are widely known as the *risk drivers*.

Risk drivers are not risks in themselves, but the potential trigger points for risk. However, they need to be set in context. For example, a room used as a study might contain several risk drivers, but depending whether it was for use by an adult or by a child, the drivers would be of lesser or greater significance. Thus, power points, electrical cabling, paper shredder, sharp corners to a desk, letter opener and stapler would be greater risk drivers for a child.

In a business project it is possible to devise focus areas for the identification of risk. These might be sections of the project to which the team can easily relate, for example, product design, product development, product testing or project resources. These make useful categories within which risk may be analysed and reported (see also Chapter 6, *Analysing and reporting risk*). Within each of the focus areas are risk drivers. Thus, a useful prelude to identifying risk would be to construct a table of potential risk drivers against each focus area. Table 2.2 gives an idea of this for a software development project.

The focus areas and risk drivers mentioned above are internal to the project. Consideration also needs to be given to external focus areas, i.e., areas outside of the project that could cause concern. Table 2.3 gives some suggestions. Many projects suffer more from problems within the business or the marketplace rather than within the project. It is all too easy to forget the wider scope when immersed in the project detail.

Identification of the focus areas and risk drivers is best done in a workshop, where team members can reach a consensus, each contributing information from their particular areas of expertise. See the section in Chapter 2 titled *The Risk Identification Workshop*.

Once the focus areas and risk drivers have been identified, the next step is to ask what can go wrong for each of the areas. I prefer to build up a risk concept

Table 2.2 Sample focus areas and risk drivers for a software development project

Focus Area	Risk Driver
Application design	Functional specification
Application coding	Version control
	Documentation
	Coding quality
	Resources
Integration testing	Test method
	Documentation
Systems testing	System performance
	Documentation
User acceptance	Test scripts
	User resources
Parallel running	Data version control
	Data consistency
	Data security
User training	Training method
	Training schedule
	Support

Table 2.3 Sample of external focus areas and risk drivers

Focus Area	Risk Driver
Business operations	User preparation
	User buy-in
	User requirements/expectations
	Quality standard
	Resources
	Security
Business organisation	Sponsorship
	Restructuring
	Cost reductions
	Office rationalisation
	Globalisation
	Business culture
Legislation	Regulatory requirements/changes
	Health and safety
	Data protection
	Employment law
Marketplace	Consumers/customers
	Suppliers
	Prices
	Mergers and acquisitions
Climate	Fire, flood, storms
Political	War, strikes, protests, terrorism
	Changes in government

map leading from the risk drivers to ever-increasing degrees of impact. Chapter 6, *Analysing and reporting risk* (*Risk modelling* section), shows some examples. An important aspect of this map is that it shows causes and impacts. As we have seen from the section *Expressing risk* in this chapter, the risk statement needs to be linked to a cause or causes, resulting in an impact.

Various inputs to the risk identification process are useful, not least:

- the project plan
    - if a plan has been constructed (i.e., the project is not in pre-planning stage), then the tasks identified on the plan are important inputs. If tasks are not yet available, then a work breakdown structure could be just as useful.
- expertise
    - gaining input from experts in particular areas of the project.
- precedence
    - input from past project experience in the company – some companies have a knowledge database, capturing lessons learned from previous projects.
- industry knowledge
    - input from similar projects in similar industries – some of this information may be proprietary, though increasingly much is now in the public domain via statutory requirements, professional bodies, etc.
- checklists
    - best-practice guidance compiled from previous project experience. Checklists of open questions tend to be less cumbersome to use and more useful than checklists of closed questions.
- simulation tools
    - many of the automated tools for identifying and assessing risk perform work on project planning software, running routines such as Monte Carlo simulation, which examines the possibility of tasks achieving their end dates. Whilst this can be of great assistance, risk identification remains primarily a human activity.

These inputs can be assessed via:

- a Risk Identification Workshop
    - taking the opportunity to get the whole team focussing on risk in one session. Whilst this is a useful forum for identifying risk, it is not practical to run this type of workshop every week. In order to embrace the continual process of identifying risk, it will be important to seek regular input from other avenues.

- interviews
  - obtaining information from team members and those external to the project.
- weekly status meetings

The Risk Identification Workshop

The best way to identify risk is via a group session. Running a Risk Identification Workshop is an excellent way of gaining team input, expertise and, importantly, buy-in to the risk management process. For this reason it is good to run such a workshop at project start-up and also, if appropriate, at client proposal stage. If it is run for the latter stage (and I suggest it should be the norm when creating client proposals of any substance) then the risks identified can be carried forward into the start-up workshop, should the contract be won. It is also good practice to run Risk Identification Workshops at the completion of major milestones.

Scope and boundaries

The Risk Identification Workshop can be run as a half-day, one-day or two-day session. Any less time than a half-day is likely to be unproductive; any more time than two days is likely to be too cumbersome for the participants.

It is important to set the boundaries before starting the workshop. My advice is to concentrate on identifying the risks rather than attempting to assess them as well. This keeps the workshop nicely contained. Identifying risks and assigning risk owners is as far as I prefer to go in one session, since it is the risk owner's job to ensure that assessment is done, and this can be done later. Assessing probability and impact in a large group can be time-consuming, involving extended debate, so a separate workshop is advisable (see the section *Risk Assessment Workshop* in Chapter 3, *Assessing risk*). Also, in order to assess risks properly, additional input is usually required, and this is not always available from the expertise in the room. However, there will inevitably be some sort of discussion concerning probability and impact, which, of course, should be captured for later use.

Input material

A useful input to the workshop will be the project plan, if available. It is possible to prioritise the tasks on the plan and merely assess the most critical of these at the workshop. Whilst this has value at subsequent Risk Identification Workshops, I feel that it is beneficial at an initial workshop to be able to step back from the detailed tasks and assess the project environment as a whole through focus areas and risk drivers.

Other useful materials might be contracts, statements of work, the project work breakdown structure and organisation breakdown structure, lists of dependencies and assumptions, the current issue log and financial breakdowns, for example. If any Monte Carlo simulation has been run, then that output would be valuable for identifying duration and cost risks.

It is usually helpful to circulate project material in advance of the workshop.

Participants

Participants for the workshop should be the core project team plus other interested parties who are able to add value to the exercise. These should include the client, where applicable, sub-contractors (working both externally and internally), sponsors, stakeholders, sales, procurement, finance, legal and HR (human resources), for example. It may not be possible to obtain a full team, but the more diverse the participants, the better the coverage will be. Having the sponsor(s) present will give encouragement to the team, even if present for only a short while.

An experienced facilitator will be required. This should not be the project manager. He or she will need the freedom to participate. A note-taker will be helpful as much of the ensuing debate could be useful later when assessing the risks. Someone will be needed to enter the risks into the risk register.

Agenda

The agenda can be fairly open within the overall time allowed. An example is shown in Table 2.4. It is useful for the project manager to give an introduction and state the background to the project. Some of the participants may be meeting for the first time, so this is a great opportunity for team building.

Table 2.4 Suggested agenda for a Risk Identification Workshop

Agenda item	*Responsibility*
Welcome and project background	Project manager
The project in a business context	Project sponsor
Introduction to the workshop process	Facilitator
Identification of focus areas	All, guided by facilitator
Identification of risk drivers	All, guided by facilitator
Identification of impacts	All, guided by facilitator
Identification of risks	All, guided by facilitator
Assignment of risk owners	All, led by project manager
Wrap-up and next steps	Project manager

Deciding the focus areas can be next on the agenda. The sub-projects, phases and divisions of the project can be a useful guide. It will probably be necessary to prioritise the focus areas in order to accommodate discussion within the time allowed for the workshop.

Next, the risk drivers can be identified. This can be accomplished to good effect by getting participants to write their suggestions and the focus area to which they apply on sticky notes, which can be arranged on a white board. With the risk drivers suitably arranged, participants can then write suggested impacts. The impacts can be arranged as a flow extending from the risk drivers, similar to the risk concept map that I describe in Chapter 6, *Analysing and reporting risk*.

Now that causes and impacts have been identified, it only remains to extract the risks. Once this has been done risk owners can be assigned. Technically, assigning risk owners is part of the risk assessment phase. However, I find it advantageous to attempt to assign them during the Risk Identification Workshop, so that you can obtain a consensus from the participants. Assigning them afterwards can be a protracted exercise.

The facilitator of the workshop should ensure that someone is able to enter the risks and the names of the risk owners into a risk register. Output from the workshop should be a set of newly identified risks, ready for assessment.

What could go wrong?

Some risk management books devote pages to the possible causes of risk. I prefer to highlight some of the more common situations that can cause risk during the lifespan of a project or programme, and let you decide how these relate to your own projects. Figure 8.1 shows some of the key influences that need to be kept in balance.

These key influences put the programme or project at risk. Some of these are internally manifested, others are external to the project and to the company. It is important to recognise these two environments – internal and external, i.e., the near and the far. The former is relatively familiar and the latter often unfamiliar.

One of these groups of influences relates to control. The importance of maintaining control cannot be overstated. Results of not maintaining control can include excessive scope creep, unmanaged resources (both in-house and sub-contractor) and a project management system that is not followed. Of course, project management is all about being in control, but it needs strength of mind and purpose in order to effect it.

Change control is a particularly good example of where strong management is needed to ensure that the process is followed. So often, I've seen good processes in place that are not being applied – the spirit is willing but the flesh is weak!

The business itself is often its own worst enemy. Legacy processes, hidden agendas, ivory towers, internal politics and bureaucracy can all hinder a project's progress. Recognising these inhibitors is part of the way to solving the problem. Building and getting agreement to a sound project management system is another part. If the project needs to run at a faster pace than business–as–usual then this must be negotiated up front. For example, a need to obtain five signatures on a travel order may be fine for normal business operations, but for a fast-moving project it is clearly not.

Existing projects may well be competing for resources and also may be on a collision course with your own project. In large companies, few individuals know exactly what other initiatives are going on outside of a particular business. A prime job of the project sponsor is to ensure that the project is not conflicting with other requirements.

The realisation of benefits may not be uppermost in the mind of a project manager when embroiled in the everyday operation of the project. However, particular project activities relate to the successful achievement of benefits, not least quality control. A good quality plan is an essential item, but many projects fail to produce one or examine the overall quality of what is being undertaken. Many concentrate just on testing, but testing is only one aspect of quality. The final proof is the acceptance of the deliverables by the client or end users. This will show whether quality has been given the correct attention.

Communication is another key requirement of project management. Benefits and quality are both influenced by good communication and the management of expectations. If these are managed well then the transfer of deliverables becomes relatively easy.

All the above are internal influences and relatively easy to manage. More difficult to manage are external events, such as market changes, government legislation or new technology. These can really stop a project in its tracks.

These and other influences are discussed further under the following relevant project stage. I've used the standard, conceptual approach to these stages, as shown in Figure 2.1 below. See also the section *Eight things to get right* in Chapter 8, *Managing risk*.

Project start-up

Project start-up is one of the most fraught periods of a project's lifespan. It is usually accompanied by frenetic activity, often against the clock. Processes need to be established, plans need to be laid, suppliers need to be engaged and the team needs to be put in place. In short, there are many risks that can occur. However, it is also a period when many future issues may be avoided, since the start-up activity should be laying the foundations for the remaining phases of the project. It is, therefore, a period of opportunity. I liken it to decorating a room

Figure 2.1 Standard project phases

of a house. The majority of the work should be in the preparation. Over, say, a 5-day period, 3.5 days should be spent on preparing the surfaces and 1.5 days for pasting and wallpapering. Shortening the preparation phase runs the risk of problems at a later date.

The risks present in the project start-up phase are often self-imposed. An example is the temptation to commence work before essential things are in place, for example supplier contracts or user requirements. The question often needing to be answered is *"How much work can be done (i.e., how much risk can be taken) without certain things in place?"* This can only be answered properly by undertaking a risk assessment. Few people do anything as formal as this, though, and so run the risk of problems later on.

Failure to complete the start-up phase to a reasonable schedule can have a very demoralising effect on staff and can contribute to a high staff turnover at what is a critical phase in a project. Having project teams wound up and displaced can rapidly spell trouble.

REQUIREMENTS SIGN-OFF

A key activity during start-up is to firm up the project requirements. It is the lynchpin for the whole project. Proceeding to work without a firm and agreed set of requirements is asking for trouble later on. *"Oh, but we always have change control"*, people often respond, to which I always reply: *"But how well do you enforce it?"* (see *Change control*, later in this chapter).

The risk of late requirements sign-off often appears on start-up risk registers. If there is any doubt about the firmness of requirements, it is usually a sign that the project is *not* ready to proceed to the design phase. The risk is more critical for fixed-price projects. If requirements and exclusions are not pinned down, there will always be arguments later.

A key question to ask during start-up is whether the project is competing against other projects trying to do similar things. So-called *collision course* projects are quite common in large companies where local initiatives are less understood across departments.

TOP-DOWN PLANNING

Another important activity during start-up is the building of the project plan. This may be the ratification of earlier estimates (such as those submitted for a client proposal) or the construction of a new plan.

Any plan that has been handed down to the project manager (top-down planning), with fixed milestones and end dates, must automatically be high risk. *"But all our projects are like this and I have no say in the key dates"* is a common objection. For me, this is not project management. The true project manager is able to influence sponsors and stakeholders concerning the plan. It is fundamental to the role.

GETTING RESOURCES AND SKILLS ON BOARD

Resource risks occurring during start-up are often related to the availability and commitment of resources, but cost and skills also feature. Establishing the right number of resources and skills seems never to be easy at start-up. If you commence work with resource deficiencies, how long can you continue before difficulties occur? Resource planning should really occur during the pre-start-up phase, allowing time for a viable team to be recruited.

Resources assigned late in the project will inevitably increase costs, either directly through the cost of sub-contractors, or indirectly through a possible decrease in productivity. A tendency towards undertaking tasks in parallel that were designed to be sequential is a symptom of late resource assignment. If work has to be compressed through the nonavailability of resources, then risk is transferred from project performance to the business operation, with the result that support and rectification costs multiply for the lower quality product delivered.

A key understanding is whether the project is competing against other projects and initiatives for particular resources. What position is the project against other things the company is doing? Is it the number one project for this year? The lower down the priority order, the less guarantee of commitment is the usual situation.

CONTRACT SIGN-OFF

Like requirements, contract sign-off often features in the risk registers of projects during the start-up phase. The danger of proceeding with work without signed contracts needs to be understood. Each company will have different practices and requirements. It usually becomes more difficult to sign contracts once work has commenced. Negotiation powers are often reduced.

Contracts need to be examined carefully to ensure that they place individual risks with the party most able to effect its management – if risks are forced on inappropriate parties trouble is almost inevitable, and in many countries may be open to legal challenge under "Unfair Contract Terms" legislation. Letters of Intent are often seen as a way to expedite a project while the contract is awaiting sign-off by one party or the other – these can be commercially extremely dangerous and, within the confines of this text, the advice is that they should not be used.

Design

The design phase of a project is usually the period when the project team is presented with the reality of the undertaking. As requirements are translated into design, so the potential for risk increases. Probability is likely to reduce but the potential impacts of any risks not eliminated may rise dramatically.

DESIGN SPECIFICATIONS SIGN-OFF

Both requirements sign-off and design sign-off are critical activities at the start-up and design phases, respectively. In a software development project this would be the sign-off of a functional specification. In a construction project this would equate to building specifications and drawings. The design phase is a good test for whether the requirements are firm. It is also a test for whether the requirements are feasible. If the requirement is for something totally new there will be no precedent for the work. Has it been done before? . . . in the company? . . . in the industry? These are relevant questions to ask when considering risk here.

In some projects there is an integrated research and development stage, such that design specifications have to be framed in terms of developing the technologies. This development stage needs to be planned, production managed, risk assessed and risk managed.

RESOURCES AND SKILLS AVAILABILITY

The design phase should give a better indication of the requirement for particular skills and resources. As with the start-up phase, their availability could give rise to risk. Commitment of resources for the required period of time is often a cause for concern, as is the general availability in the marketplace of a particular skill. Compare the use of new oil field technology offshore, where no pool of uncommitted, competent operatives exists to date, to a standard house-building project, where a widespread pool of skilled resource is available.

Where in-house resources are not available, sub-contracted resources may be an option. These require advance planning and cost approvals. Managing the cost of sub-contracted resources effectively is no mean task.

Build

As work gets underway, the unfamiliar becomes the familiar, and many of the risks identified in earlier phases are lessened or cease to be relevant. Component production risks, for example, are closed out after their build is complete. This is not to say that the build phase is not without risk. New risks can be identified, many of which may test the resilience of the schedule and the quality systems.

CHANGE CONTROL

Change control is one of those processes that looks great on paper but is often difficult to accomplish in practice. The danger is that acceptance of small changes outside of the change control procedure contributes to scope creep. Much depends on the culture of the company. Some companies are able to enforce change control, whilst others have a more loose interpretation of changes and usually suffer as a result. Some projects undoubtedly have slack in the schedule in which to accommodate small changes, but if changes are accepted outside of a formal process there is no ability to add up the knock-on effect of incremental change and the changes created in the overall picture of risk. For example, changing a value in a line of code in a software programme may seem innocent enough, but its effect on dependent code could be significant.

EXPECTATION MANAGEMENT

Ensuring a match between requirements and expectation is an important activity for any project. So many projects have foundered because the outcome did not meet customer expectations. The solutions may have been technically elegant, but if they are not what the end users need or can use then they have clearly failed. Again, clarity and agreement as to what is excluded from the project scope should be established from the earliest stages of project initiation.

Contributing to risks of poor customer or user expectation are poor communications management and poor quality management. In order to reduce the surprise element to users of what is to be delivered, there needs to be regular communication and involvement. Prototyping is one of many opportunities for users to gain a "hands-on" view of deliverables and user involvement in the quality assurance processes is vital.

Key questions to ask are:

- What opportunities are planned for end user communication and sign-off? Requirements? Design? Materials checks? Prototypes? Usability test? Acceptance test?
- How are end users to be involved in the project? For reviews and feedback? For quality assurance? As testers?
- Do the project executors fully understand how the deliverable is to be used and exploited by the end users?

Test

The testing of products, whether as a discrete phase or alongside development, is a typical breeding ground for risk. The predictability of outcomes is often difficult, such that a period set aside for testing is frequently over-run. This can have a knock-on effect on other projects waiting to use the test facilities.

If there is pressure to curtail testing, in order, for example, to meet a particular deadline, then the risk of post-implementation failure must be greater. Also, additional costs may be expended in support.

RESOURCES AND SKILLS AVAILABILITY

Resources for testing always seem to be difficult to obtain. Planning their availability in advance may give some assurance, but there are often problems marshalling them on the actual dates required. The administrative workload in scheduling resources to test plans is often underestimated. Also, in the event of a problem, it may be difficult to obtain specialist resources for rectification purposes.

TEST ENVIRONMENT

The availability of specialist test environments and tools is often a cause for concern. Has the test environment itself been tested, so that when it needs to be used on an appointed day everything works?

Is the team clear on what types of testing are required? For example, this could include unit (component) testing, regression testing, stress testing, structural testing, volume testing, integration testing, fire safety testing, client acceptance testing or usability testing.

TEST RESULTS

Predicting the outcome of tests is itself often high risk. In a software development project that has a discrete testing phase, errors in the code will be logged daily, but decisions about whether to continue testing may not be taken until the end of each week. A two-week acceptance test, therefore, could easily last six weeks.

In a product development project much will depend on the nature of the tests being carried out. Stress testing of engineered components, for example, is more likely to be predictable in outcome than usability testing, which is notorious for revealing the unexpected.

Hand-over

Hand-over can be formal or informal, depending on the nature of the project. Formal hand-overs often require certificates of acceptance, but even informal hand-overs need some form of recognition of the transition from project to business-as-usual. It is an area subject to potential confusion between project team and client, particularly concerning the boundary of transition from say, project support to operational support.

USER PREPAREDNESS

The readiness of the user organisation to receive the deliverables is often a focus for risk. If expectations have been set regularly throughout the project then the risk of nonacceptance is lessened. A question to ask is: "*How prepared is the user organisation in terms of training, support, facilities, business processes and user documentation, for the change being delivered?*"

Where the deliverable is a physical product, unscheduled costs and risks may be incurred by the receiving organisation with the unexpected delivery of the product (manning, storage and insurance, for example), for which the organisation may seek reimbursement.

BENEFITS

Hand-over should include the provision for monitoring the effectiveness of the changes implemented. In a programme this is the role of the Business Change Manager, but for a stand-alone project the role needs to be specified, probably within the user community. The risk of nonachievement of benefits depends on many factors, not least user take-up. Benefits will accrue over time, but unless a measurement process is in place the original project sponsors will not see how their investment has been realised.

For certain projects, the benefit achievement can only be delivered by the integrated delivery of a programme (e.g., a new warehouse facility which integrates building, IT systems, staff recruitment and training projects).

3   Assessing risk

Once a risk has been identified it needs to be assessed for its likelihood of occurrence and its possible impact. This is where the real science of risk management comes into play.

In order to assess a risk you need good data. In particular, you need to know about:

- the environment in which the risk has occurred
- the environment it may impact
- whether the risk has occurred before:
  - in your project
  - in your business
  - in your industry
- how the risk was treated and the effect of that treatment

At a general level you will need basic data regarding your project, such as the overall cost of the project in terms of people and resources, and the approximate daily value of keeping the project going. This is so that any impact that represents a delay to the project can be adequately calculated.

Less easy to calculate are any indirect costs, such as:

- lost sales
- lost opportunities
- loss of market position and/or share
- liquidated damages payable to a client

Notwithstanding this, assessment is very much a perception, and being a perception it is subject to a large margin of error.

This is why it is always helpful to record comments concerning the assessment of any risk. The perception at the time the risk was assessed may differ from later assessments. By recording comments at the time of assessment, later assessors can see why a risk was rated as a particular probability or impact. If conditions have changed, then a new rating can be applied.

Chapter 5, *Recording risk*, shows the detailed fields in the assessment layer of a standard risk register. You may find it helpful to review this with the text below.

Risk assessment comprises various sub-phases:

* assignment of risk owners
* estimating probability and impact
* assessing uncertainty (through risk exposures, for example)
* assigning priorities

Assigning risk owners

Each risk on the risk register needs to have ownership. This ensures that it is not just something recorded, but that someone is actively working to ensure that it is assessed, reassessed and a response plan prepared.

Not many projects seem to bother with assigning owners for individual risks. I think this is poor practice. Making someone accountable for a risk ensures that it is not left unattended and that it has a chance of being properly assessed. Assigning an owner also directs responsibility to the person most skilled to assess the risk. Leaving this to the person who raised the risk or to the project manager is not necessarily effective, unless the raiser happens to be the ideal candidate for risk owner. It is not always easy to assign a risk owner, but should at least be attempted. In my experience, risks without risk owners are often the ones that are left without actions.

The project manager would assign a risk owner once a risk has been identified. The risk owner should be someone who has some affinity with the risk. It is often the person who raised the risk, but not exclusively. In this case, that person has a vested interest in ensuring that the risk is suitably dealt with. A risk owner may own more than one risk. This is particularly useful where risks are related or interdependent. A risk owner may own a complete category of risks, such as all risks relating to marketing or cable laying.

The role of the risk owner is described in the section *Risk roles* in Chapter 7, *Administering risk*.

Estimating probability and impact

Assessment is primarily concerned with assessing the probability of the risk occurring and its impact to the project. These are the elements that are highly subjective. Even if there is data to support a previous occurrence in a similar situation on a similar project, the calculation of probability can only be a rough estimate. Because of this, many project teams assess probability and impact merely as high, medium or low. I feel this is so vague and noncommittal that it is really not worth doing. Even with the margin of error I prefer to use a much finer granularity, and so recommend the use of percentages.

In Chapter 6, *Analysing and reporting risk*, I show how probability and impact can be used to monitor risk and to report it.

Probability

For rating probability, I suggest using a percentage. This is much better than using high, medium and low as ratings. In percentage terms, "high" would equate to a figure of anything from between 67% and 99%, which leaves a considerable margin of error. A probability of 70% ought to be quite different from that of 90%, and to rate them both as merely "high" and, therefore, treating them as similar in probability terms, is not good practice.

You will notice that I refrained from using 100% as a probability. This is because I view a risk with a 100% probability as an event that is definitely going to take place, i.e., as a future issue and not as a risk. Consider, for example, a risk of government legislation being passed that would impact your project. There is no doubt that a risk should be raised in this case. However, if the legislation has already been passed, but will not come into effect until a fixed date in the future, that is not a risk but an issue. There is no risk that the legislation will not happen, so the project will have to take immediate action to avert the impact. (See also *Differences between risks and issues* in Chapter 2, *Identifying and expressing risk*.)

What equates to high, medium and low in terms of probability is subject to debate. Some risk managers would say that anything above a 40% probability is high risk and deserves a priority response. Some would argue that probabilities above 50% should be treated as certainties in terms of action response. Whatever view you might favour, it is important that everyone in the team understands the meaning of the probability thresholds you wish to set.

Attempting to estimate a probability between 1% and 99% can be quite daunting for those not used to having to assess against such a large range. My recommendation is not to be too concerned about the initial assessment of probability, since, over time, as more people see the risk and discuss it and more data becomes available, the percentage can be refined. Probability will come under closer scrutiny when people start to consider seriously the cost of impact.

I remember, when assessing for a company the overall risk impact of the implementation of the Euro currency, that the team's initial estimate of impact was higher than the final estimate. What was driving this estimate was probability. It was being used in a multiplier to estimate the contingency fund in case problems arose on E-day. Once people started to question the accuracy of the probability estimate, new data was sought and it was refined accordingly. In this case, the probability decreased – not just as a result of new data but also as a result of the work being done to respond to the risks.

Many probability estimates reflect an unfamiliarity of work to be performed. As a project team begins to execute the work, confidence usually builds and probability estimates decrease. Of course, this does not always happen!

A key influencer in assessing probability is a person's attitude to risk. Everyone on a project team will have a different view of what is risky and what isn't, as well as a different view of the chance of a risk occurring. A project manager will quickly understand this through regular engagement with the team and needs to take a responsible combined view of the output from any risk assessment.

Impact

For me, impact is mainly an expression of cost and is best assessed in monetary units. I know there are other ways in which it can be expressed, such as in terms of productivity. Ultimately, however, it leads to a cost – a cost that has a direct link to the project budget.

When assessing impact, I like to think of the repair cost of the damage caused. For some projects this is an obvious physical thing, such as a pipe burst. In business and IT projects, for example, it is often nonphysical, and usually relates to time lost. In physical impacts a repair cost could also be a replacement cost, if the object cannot be repaired. In nonphysical projects the repair cost could also be a contingency or workaround cost, if no more time could be squeezed from the schedule in order to make the repair.

This is basically how insurance companies work when underwriting risk. Sophisticated tables are used to calculate probabilities and an estimate to repair is made based on a replacement price with allowance for wear and tear in many cases. The level of sophistication needed for your project will be dictated by the nature of your project and your company standards.

Sometimes the cost of repair may relate to a more indirect cost, such as loss of life, loss of sales and revenue. These will be more difficult to estimate. Expressing impact as a repair cost is a good basic approach, however.

Additionally, I like to express the impact cost as a percentage of the project budget. This really puts a focus on the risk in relation to the project as a whole. A risk with an impact of 110% of project budget would certainly get some attention at the weekly project status meeting!

Table 3.1 gives an example of some of the types of impact against types of repair cost.

Using "time delay" as an example, the chart shows that the repair cost relates to the cost of retaining all or part of the project team for an additional period. This is the most common form of impact repair. It could, for example, arise from a sub-team overrunning, thus holding up the next stage of work. In this case, the repair cost might be three resources at £1500 per week for three additional weeks, being a total of £4,500. If the probability of the impact occurring is set at 60%, then the risk exposure is £2,700 (£4500 x 60%). The next section, *Assessing uncertainty*, gives more information on calculating a risk exposure.

Some impacts could be so damaging to a project that a contingency plan needs to be put in place. When assessing impacts it is always worth considering their criticality. "*Could the project survive if a particular risk impacted?*" is a question worth asking of every risk. If the answer is no, then a contingency plan might need to be drawn up. Contingency plans are discussed in Chapter 4, *Responding to risk*.

Some impacts are difficult to justify. I once noticed a risk in a company risk register that stood out significantly from all the others. It was expressed as "risk of damage to company reputation". It had been assessed as 70% probability and £230m impact. I asked the team involved whether they really believed the high assessment. They all concurred. I warned them that senior management would

Table 3.1 Example of types of repair cost to risk impacts

Type of Impact	Typical Reason	Type of Repair Cost
Time delay	Incorrect estimates of workload; unexpected additional work	The cost of retaining all or part of the project team for the required repair time.
Contingency	Impact would be devastating to the project and the likelihood of impact would be too high to risk any damage occurring	The cost of supplying or reserving something in case a risk impacts. Money set aside in case of impact.
Resource/skill shortage	Holidays, sickness, skill deficiency	The cost of hiring an additional resource for a required time period.
Benefits impact	Likelihood that certain benefits may not be met	The cost of respecifying the existing requirements, plus any compensation to a client for benefits not met.
Marketing impact	Risk that user communities or the general public do not fully understand the deliverables	The cost of additional external or internal marketing and end user support.
Travel impact	The need for travelling may have been underestimated	The cost of additional travel and associated accommodation.
Training/support impact	Feelings that training or support may not be adequate	The cost of specifying and supplying additional training or support, if necessary.

certainly quiz them on this risk, it being so significant, and suggested that they try to understand the nature of the reputation damage and its underlying causes. I recommended they construct a cause-and-effect diagram for this purpose. This they did, but clearly struggled in finding solid reasons for their fears. The diagram showed that much of their fear was unfounded and that they had over-estimated both the probability and the impact. They consequently reduced the risk exposure, making the risk less significant.

This shows the power of the cause-and-effect diagram as a means of testing assessments and underlying fears. It is particularly good for assessing unspecific impacts. See Chapter 6, *Analysing risk*, for guidance in constructing a cause-and-effect diagram.

Assessing uncertainty

Once data is gathered for probability and impact, it is possible to assess it for creating a picture of uncertainty. The combination of probability and impact allows decisions to be made regarding the risk priority, its effect on the project and the most appropriate ways to treat it. Much of this assessment is based on perceptions: the current state of the project, appetite for risk, precedence, etc. Two technical ways of assessing uncertainty are *risk exposure* and *EMV* (expected monetary value). The latter is a product of the former. Used together they can present a powerful statement of uncertainty. The section *Dealing with uncertainty* in Chapter 8, *Managing risk*, gives more information on the nontechnical aspects of uncertainty assessment.

Calculating the risk exposure

For me, one of the most important aspects of risk assessment is the *risk exposure*. Any senior manager requesting base information about a project needs to know at least three figures: (i) the project cost; (ii) the project benefit; and (iii) the risk exposure.

Compare the following three projects:

Project	Cost	Benefit	Risk Exposure
1. Replace sales order system	£0.5m	£3m savings, years 1 to 3	£0.2m
2. New product offering	£0.5m	£6m revenue, year 1	£1.8m
3. New accounting system	£3m	£12m savings, years 1 to 3	£5m

Without the risk exposure information, Project 3 looks attractive. With the risk exposure, however, it looks much less attractive. Although the risk exposure is relevant for only the life of the project, it could significantly dent the perceived benefit. As a decision-making tool, risk exposure is a vital component. Even though there may be a large margin of error in its calculation, risk exposure is a powerful criterion when used in comparing projects.

In its simplest form, risk exposure (RE) is calculated by multiplying the impact repair cost (IRC) by the percentage probability of occurrence (P). Thus, £IRC x P% = £RE. The risk exposures for each risk are added to form a total for the whole project.

The overall risk exposure is, of course, reduced by the effect of mitigating actions. So, in calculating the risk exposure for a project at, say, pre-contract stage, it is logical to add in the effect of potential actions (reduction in probability and reduction in impact). If, for example, a project RE is calculated to be £120,000, but feasible actions can be taken to reduce that to £25,000, then the mitigated risk exposure (MRE) becomes £25,000. The cost of actions needs to be added, however. If the cost of the actions is £5,000, then the total MRE is, therefore, £30,000. The total £MRE can be added to the project budget.

Some project managers like to apply weightings to particular types of impact or priority of risk. These can increase or reduce the risk exposure. However the final result is calculated, it is important to remember that the result is only a guideline, a comfort factor and, at best, a form of comparison. It is certainly better than nothing and, when project experience is fed back into the equation, it can improve in accuracy year on year.

Companies practising corporate management of change through strategically aligned programmes would probably want to set a company standard for the calculation of risk exposure. Such an accounting convention would enable the company to roll up the risk exposures of programmes and their constituent projects in order to plan its annual budgets for corporate change.

Calculating EMV

Expected monetary value is an accounting method that represents the outcome of positive and negative figures in a range of worst case, most likely and best case. Given that there is a significant margin of error in the calculation of a risk exposure, it is logical to present the result not as a single figure but as a range of figures. EMV also allows for both the threat and opportunity side of risk to be included. In the example below, there are two risks, one a threat and one an opportunity, both estimated to worst case, most likely and best case results:

Threat/ Opportunity	Probability	Impact	£RE Worst Case	£RE Most Likely	£RE Best Case
Component is delivered late	50%	£15K	£15K	£7.5K	£0K
Design is signed off early	30%	£20K	£0K	-£6K	-£20K
EMV			**£15K**	**£1.5K**	**-£20K**

The most likely case is the risk exposure for the risk or opportunity. The worst case is the full impact amount for a threat or no reward for an opportunity. The best case is zero for a threat (i.e., the risk does not impact) or the full reward for an opportunity. EMV is the total of all the threats and opportunities. In the table above, the best case is that the project profits by £20K. The worst case is that the project carries an estimated total loss of £15K.

Note the signs are reversed for positive and negative. This reflects a project budgetary position, where money is added for risk, but taken away for opportunities. For example, if the project has a baseline budget of £500K, the best case removes £20K from that budget, lowering it to £480K. This accounts for the opportunity of the design being signed off early. The worst-case picture adds £15K to the baseline, making it £515K. Risk exposure and EMV allow new budget baselines to be constructed to reflect all risk (both the positive opportunity and the negative threat). Note that these examples are unmitigated. In reality you would want to apply mitigating actions to improve the figures before applying them to any budget. See Chapter 4, *Responding to risk*, for guidance on assigning actions.

Setting risk priorities

Having identified a list of risks, it is helpful to know which ones to tackle first. Severity of impact is probably the best criterion to help decide, though other factors need to be considered as well.

The urgency of a risk is one such factor. Any impact that is imminent would need to be dealt with urgently, depending on the severity of its impact. Often there are critical windows for actions, so while a risk impact may be some time away, the opportunity to manage it effectively might be imminent.

You may find it useful to construct a matrix of probability against impact so that you can see more easily which risks to prioritise for assigning actions. (See the section *Examples of risk charts* in Chapter 6, *Analysing and reporting risk*, for an example.)

Priorities can be set in several ways. High, medium or low is a common three-fold representation. Some projects prefer to use priority numbers – anything from priority 1 and 2 up to 6. It is important to ensure that everyone understands what the priorities mean. High, medium, low or 1, 2, 3 need to be qualified. I prefer to keep the levels of priority to a minimum and find that two levels are usually adequate. Thus:

Priority 1	Risks that will seriously damage the project if they impact
Priority 2	Risks that will have a contained effect on the project but will not seriously damage it.

This rating caters for both urgency and severity. It is simple and easy to remember. However, I recognise that for certain technical projects being managed to close tolerances a finer granularity is desirable.

Don't be tempted to ignore risks that are low in impact cost. Even little impacts, if they occur excessively, frequently can accumulate and increase the overall risk exposure.

The Risk Assessment Workshop

In large projects it may be desirable to hold a group session to determine the assessment of risks identified in a previous session. More accurate assessments can usually be obtained through such a session, since participants are dedicating themselves to a single aim. A Risk Assessment Workshop is valuable for risks requiring input from several parties, where assessment can be debated and argued. Risk owners will have a key role to play in the workshop, since they will have gathered base material for discussion concerning the risks they own.

Scope and boundaries

The Risk Assessment Workshop can be run as a half-day, one-day or two-day session. Any less time than half a day is likely to be unproductive. Any more time than two days is likely to be too cumbersome for the participants. It is important to set the boundaries before starting the workshop. The workshop performs both the activities of assessment and risk response. The output of the workshop, therefore, would be a set of fully assessed risks plus suggestions and actions for responding to them, including ownership of those actions.

On a two-day workshop it can be useful to arrange for the overnight production of the formal documentation of the results of the first day's work.

Participants

Participants for the workshop should be the core project team plus other interested parties who are able to contribute. This should include the client, as applicable, sub-contractors (working both externally and internally), sponsors, stakeholders, sales, procurement, finance, legal and HR (human resources), for example. It may not be possible to obtain a full team, but the more diverse the participants are the better the coverage will be. Don't forget that perception will be a key factor in assessing probability and impact, so attention to participants' risk attitude will be important for the project manager.

An experienced facilitator will be required. This should not be the project manager. He or she will need the freedom to participate. A note-taker will be helpful, as much of the ensuing debate could be useful later when assessing the risks. Someone will be needed to enter the risks into the risk register.

Particular experts will need to be identified before the workshop if their input is needed for assessment and risk response. These may well be people from outside of the core team.

Agenda

The agenda can be fairly open within the overall time allowed. An example is shown in Table 3.2. It is useful for the project manager to give an introduction on the current state of the project prior to the introduction of the workshop process by the facilitator.

The current risk register should be distributed to all attendees prior to the workshop. The first step is to undertake an initial prioritisation of the risks in the risk register. This can only be a quick assessment, since in order to undertake prioritisation fully one needs to know the probabilities and impacts, which will only be done later in the workshop. This initial priority is so that the risks can be assessed in order of importance. If the number of risks to assess is small then they do not need to be broken down further. If the number is large then it is useful to break down the risks into sub-groupings, either by type, by focus area or by risk owner.

Table 3.2 Suggested agenda for a Risk Assessment Workshop

Agenda item	Responsibility
1. Welcome and project status	Project manager
2. Introduction to the workshop process	Facilitator
3. Quick prioritisation of risks in the risk register	All, guided by facilitator
4. Identification of risk probabilities for high priority risks	All, guided by risk owners
5. Identification of impact costs for high priority risks	All, guided by risk owners
6. Calculation of risk exposures	All, guided by facilitator
7. Reprioritisation of risks	All, led by project manager
8. Identification of response actions for high priority risks	All, guided by risk owners
9. Repeat of 4–6 for the next order of priority	All, guided by risk owners
10. Wrap-up and next steps	Project manager

The next step is to decide on the probability of occurrence for each of the risks in each category, starting with the highest priority. Then the cost of impacts can be assessed, followed by the reprioritisation of the risks.

Starting with the highest priority risks, suggestions for response actions may be taken next. The risk owners should lead this step ideally, identifying experts who can give input. If time permits, risks in the next order of priority may be assessed.

The facilitator of the workshop should ensure that someone is able to update the risks in the risk register and that any issues identified are entered in the issues log.

4   Responding to risk

Clearly, the most important aspect of risk management is the response to risks that have been identified. Yet, this is probably the least well-done of all the risk management activities. Several things work against the adequate response to risk.

Firstly, there is capacity. Risk response is not usually an activity that can be done instantly. It requires concentrated thought.

Secondly, there is cost. There are usually costs associated with carrying out risk response actions. The feasibility of these has to be weighed against the severity of the risk and the likelihood of occurrence.

Thirdly, there is the concept of probability: "*If we do nothing, will things really be as bad as we have assessed?*"

Fourthly, there is schedule. Identifying response actions adds tasks and, therefore, time to the project schedule. Risk response is usually not budgeted at the outset of the project. Some response actions may need to come under project change control.

Fifthly, there is expertise. One person is unlikely to have the expertise required to respond to all the risks. Input from various quarters will be necessary.

Sixthly, there is commitment needed to carry out the required response actions. Commitment to response actions should be as great as to the tasks on the project schedule, but many people will find themselves under time pressure and will not always be able to fulfil the actions.

Understanding the capacity, cost, probability, schedule, expertise and commitment of adequately responding to risks is one of the routes to successful risk management.

Deciding response actions

Project managers are traditionally concerned with the attributes of time, cost and quality. In a project, a risk impact usually means cost. It could also mean time and quality, of course, but even these attributes can often be translated into cost. Extending or losing time costs money and achieving quality also costs money. You could argue that projects or programmes with an immutable end date, such as calendar-related events, have "time" as an end point. With few exceptions, date-restricting events can be moved, though probably not without cost. The

European Central Bank could have moved the start date for the introduction of the Euro currency, for example, but the cost of doing so would have been significant.

In a programme, the impact end points can be more subtle. Loss of business reputation can feature regularly, and this can translate into lost revenue. A threat of litigation is another regular impact these days, and can translate into significant cost.

It is important to bear in mind the ultimate impact points when deciding response actions. These should steer your direction so that you take the most appropriate courses of action.

The persons most suited to recommend response actions are the risk owners (see *Assigning risk owners* in Chapter 3, *Assessing risk*, and *Risk roles* in Chapter 7, *Administering risk*). Their expertise can ensure that the most appropriate actions are devised with the most appropriate persons allocated to carry them out. Their recommendations, however, need to be set in the context of the project as a whole. The project manager, therefore, will need to approve any actions, as he or she is the budget holder.

Assuming the prerequisites of expressing and assessing risk have been done, the first step is to decide what type of response action is appropriate to tackle the risk. Table 4.1 gives some examples. A common action is to try and mitigate the risk for impact and probability. Mitigate just means "lessen in severity", but this is not always the most appropriate form of action. You might want to accept the risk, avoid it or insure against it, for example, rather than merely reduce its impact or the chances of it occurring.

If you accept that the risk could occur, you might want to counter its impact by specifying a contingency plan. For example, a risk that an in-house test facility may not be available within a particular time period might be countered by reserving an off-site test facility (see action A1604001 in Table 4.1). The cost of cancelling a reservation if it is not eventually required is likely to be a small price to pay for having the assurance of a contingency.

Contingency plans are often specified alongside other response actions. So, in the example above, we might also wish to specify an action to tackle the risk of the in-house facility not being available, as in action A1604002 in Table 4.1.

Contingency actions are usually specified where the damage of the impact cannot be tolerated. The probability of the risk occurring may only be very low, but should it occur the project needs a backup solution. In cases of low probability it may not be worth specifying any action to tackle the probability, so it is acceptable to tackle only the impact. This is often referred to as *active acceptance*, as opposed to *passive acceptance*, which is not responding to either the probability or the impact.

Responding to risk is time-consuming. There are no shortcuts to doing it well, so you need to be able to relate the effort required to the end result. So often, I have seen actions specified that would clearly have little or no effect on the risk, either in terms of reducing its impact or reducing its likelihood of occurrence. To me, such actions are a waste of effort. When deciding actions, it is important

Table 4.1 Risk register extract for actions

Action No.	Response Action	Action Owner	Priority	Due Date	Reduction in Prob. %	Reduction in Impact %	Cost £K	Action Status
A1604001	Make a reservation on an off-site test facility	EGH	1	01 May	0	10	3.5	02.05 Done
A1604002	Check detailed schedule with in-house test facility manager and identify gaps	EGH	2	25 April	10	0	0	02.05 Gaps in test schedule but test ready date not yet certain

to specify only actions that will have a real effect on the risk. One way to check this is to estimate the amount of reduction in impact and/or probability that the action will achieve.

In Table 4.1, the reduction in impact and probability has been estimated for each action if it is carried out successfully. Action A1604001 would have no effect on reducing the percentage probability, which was originally estimated at 50%. If the original estimate of impact was 10% of the total project cost, action A1604001 would remove the threat of impact entirely. Contingency actions usually have costs associated with them, so the cost of undertaking the action has to be added to the risk exposure. In this example, the cost of undertaking the action is £3,500.

Conversely, action A1604002 indicates that the risk owner believes 10% of the probability could be reduced by carrying out the action. So, once this action has been completed, the project manager would expect to reduce the overall probability of the risk occurring from 50% to 40%. Action A1604002 indicates no effect on the impact. This is because the action is only to check the status of something and not to reduce the damage that might occur if it impacts.

Indicating the reduction in probability and impact helps to select which actions should take priority, i.e., the ones that will have the most effect. It also shows whether additional actions are needed to reduce the impact or probability further. More importantly, it acts as an effective check on the validity of actions, and so prevents time being wasted.

Some actions will be preparatory actions for larger, more effective actions. These are often actions that require someone to find out or check something, as we have seen in the example of A1604002 in Table 4.1. They will consequently have no effect on impact or probability, but are nonetheless important. In the example above, A1604002 could be considered a preparatory action for the first action, even though some reduction in probability is indicated, i.e., *check the in-house testing schedule and if it is really not suitable then carry out the contingency plan.* The contingency plan effectively takes care of the risk impact, but it is a relatively expensive option. The project manager would probably prefer to respond to the risk by other means. The second action does not reduce the risk sufficiently, however, so other actions would need to be specified.

Sometimes a risk bears such consequences that the aspect to which it relates becomes untenable. This means that an alternative solution is required, so that the risk may be avoided. Avoiding risks in its simplest term means finding a workaround, but could easily mean a major change to a project's direction. It is fairly common in research and development (R&D), software development and other innovatory projects to need to avoid risks. Similarly, projects may need to avoid risks if the product being developed proves to carry too much risk. The section *Risk as opportunity* in Chapter 8, *Managing risk*, describes how to turn adversity into opportunity.

Another method of dealing with risk is to insure against it. This is popular in the construction industry, where insurers are accustomed to providing cover for particular types of construction risk. Insuring against a risk does not prevent it happening, but it does provide some compensation if it impacts. In many ways, it is like a contingency action. There is always a cost involved (the premium cost) and it usually relates to a project critical situation.

Table 4.2 shows a summary of the more common types of risk response strategies that you may want to employ. It also shows some sample actions. Various industries may have their own specifics – the insurance industry, for example.

Table 4.2 Summary of the more common types of risk response strategies and actions

Risk response strategy	Description	Example of action
Investigative	Actions that gather information or check the existence of something. These actions may or may not reduce the probability. They rarely reduce the impact, unless the investigation reveals, for example, that the impact would not be as severe as estimated.	Find out how many suppliers are consistently late in delivery.
	These actions are usually the first form of response actions to take. Good risk management benefits from good data.	
Acceptance	For a *passive* acceptance, response actions might monitor a situation to see whether the risk has changed in nature.	Formally review the risk at weekly progress meetings.
	For an *active* acceptance, contingency plans might be crafted (see next row).	

(Continued)

Table 4.2 (Continued)

Risk response strategy	Description	Example of action
Contingency	Actions designed to avoid or reduce the *impact* of a risk.	For a risk that a power supply might not be totally reliable during a peak operating period, a contingency might be to arrange backup power.
Mitigation	Actions that reduce either the probability or the impact or both. They are often suggested following the result of an investigative action.	For a risk that some employees might not be aware of the company health and safety guidelines, an action might be to remind employees of the guidelines and confirm that they have read them.
Avoid	Actions designed to avoid a risk by working around it. These actions may reduce both the probability and impact. They can also cause project changes. They are frequently suggested following the result of an investigative action.	For a risk that a contractor may not be able to achieve the desired finish when building a retaining wall in a particular brick, an avoiding action might be to source an alternative brick.
Transfer	Actions that transfer the risk to a third party, under contract or warranty, for example.	For a risk of insufficient in-house resource to respond to possible high demand for information concerning a new product, engage a specialist support service to whom information requests can be directed.
Opportunity	An action that seeks to turn a threat into an opportunity. Opportunity responses also often present themselves when seeking to avoid risks.	For a risk that a key supplier might default on a production owing to cash-flow problems, an opportunity might arise to form an investment partnership with the supplier.

See Chapter 5, *Recording risk*, for information on recording actions in the project risk register and Chapter 7, *Administering risk*, for information regarding the roles of the action owner and risk owner.

Managing assumptions

Most projects proceed on a basis of assumptions. Requirements and scope, in particular, are usually full of assumptions. Decisions during the course of a project are made against this background of assumptions, and the hope is that the project assumptions can eventually be turned into actualities, so that more assured decisions can be made.

The problem for risk management is that, in responding to risk, actions are often being decided against assumptions. So a validation needs to be made against the data being presented before an action is agreed. For example, is the data reliable? Where did it come from? Who agreed it? What precedent is there for making the assumption?

Many assumptions made pre-contract are able to be ratified post-contract. For a fixed-price contract this is especially desirable. Thus, for example, an assumption that a product will be developed and rolled out to 200 retail branch offices should be ratified in the statement of requirement. If it is not, and many projects proceed on the basis of unratified assumptions, then there is a risk that the assumption is incorrect. In many cases, the change control process will support such changes to the project requirements, but small assumptions that tend to compound other assumptions are often not captured by this process.

Assumptions need to be regularly tested for validity. Unless assumptions are formally logged they could be interpreted as fact by anyone needing to use them. For example, in an IT project a business analyst may make an assumption about a user requirement. A software designer may take that assumption and build it into a system design. A software programmer may use that assumption to write code. A test writer may use it to design a test program. The test designer could interpret the assumption as fact, since it has been through many hands before it reaches him or her.

The risk of response actions being invalidated through incorrect assumptions has to be recognised as a distinct possibility. Risk owners, in particular, need to be aware of changes occurring to assumptions used to mitigate the risks they own.

Managing response actions

Day-to-day administrative management of response actions is often vested in the Project Office. This would comprise checking due dates and chasing action owners for responses, recording progress and ensuring that the status of risks is generally maintained. If web-enabled interactive software is installed, then action owners and risk owners should be able to receive reminder emails of approaching and overdue action dates. Reports of overdue dates may be produced for the project manager, together with analyses of impacts to the project resulting from any overdue actions.

At what point is a risk considered fully mitigated? When do you close a risk? What do you do if a risk impacts? These are commonly asked questions about managing response actions.

Some risks are never closed, and remain on the risk register throughout a project's life. This is usually because an element of risk always remains. Response actions may have reduced the risk to the lowest level of severity, but cannot entirely eradicate it. Some risks may be closed if actions are able to eliminate it. Some risks are closed because they are no longer relevant (for example, design delay risks can be closed out at the completion of a design phase). Some risks may be closed because they have impacted, so they need to be transferred to the issues register. If all your risks, issues and changes are maintained in the same software application this is relatively easy to effect.

Some risks may be transferred to other risks, either existing or new. This happens if a risk changes in nature and becomes bound up with a similar risk, or it is thought better to open a new risk to reflect the new circumstances. The original risk is consequently closed.

Regular review of actions progress will decide whether additional actions are needed for a particular risk. Actions have a tendency to breed further actions, so it is important to ensure that the original actions are effective.

Contingency actions need particular review. They are in place in case a risk impacts, but there is no point in having a disaster recovery plan if it has not been tested. *Will the contingency plan actually work?* is a key question to ask.

Consider the following risk:

> *Because of the proposed change to employees' working conditions, there is a risk that there will be widespread rejection of the proposals, resulting in several legal claims against the company.*

Any attempt to change working conditions has to be high risk, so some form of contingency plan would be appropriate. However, until the change is announced the reactions from employees will not be fully known. How do you, therefore, respond to such a risk?

Firstly, more information needs to be gathered. Initial actions would need to concentrate on this. The possible areas of objection need to be estimated. There may be previous data for this from other areas of the company or externally – other companies have certainly gone through this activity. Also, the potential damage needs to be estimated – best case, worst case and most likely case. Then, depending on the answer, the risk may be covered by a contingency plan or may be contained through other courses of action, such as the preparation of sample responses to possible objections, bound up in a communications plan, perhaps. Further data is likely to be required, legal counsel may need to be sought and it may be necessary to test reactions through a confidential sample of employees affected.

Of course, many of these actions should appear as tasks on a project schedule. They consume time and resources. Failure to include any form of action on a project schedule may result in scope creep – the incremental enlargement of the project scope – whereby time and cost could overrun.

This example shows, firstly, how important it is to devise a plan for actions, rather than just assigning actions in a piecemeal fashion, and secondly, how important is the link between response actions and tasks on the project schedule.

Effect on the project plan

Each risk action carries a trade-off. No action is for free and the project plan will be impacted in some way. There is only so much time and money available for performing response actions and undertaking project tasks. A balance has to be made.

Things to consider are:

- the effort required to undertake the response action
- the cost required to undertake the response action
- the cost of not undertaking the response action (opportunity to avoid future issues may be lost)
- the effect on other work for the person undertaking the response action
- the importance of the response action
- how effective the response action will be (success rate in reducing the risk)
- possible savings to be made in the project budget or schedule through undertaking the response action

In some cases a change request may be required in order to effect the response action. In other cases negotiation will be required with other project stakeholders, organisations, mandatory authorities or departments beyond the organisation's project team.

I prefer to mark tasks on the project schedule that specifically relate to risk response actions. This ties them back to the risk register, so that if any changes are made on the risk register they can be easily identified and changed on the schedule. I know of no software currently that provides an automatic link between the risk register and the schedule.

5 Recording risk

Once risks have been identified it is important to be able to refer to them again, so some sort of recording mechanism needs to be established. The *risk register* is the generally accepted term for the place where risks are recorded, and the *risk log* is usually the one-line summary of each risk. You will occasionally find the two terms interchangeable, but it is good practice to refer to the detailed record as the *register* and the summary record as the *log*.

The risk register

What should a project or programme risk register look like?

Well, there are many opinions, and these will often relate to particular company practice. Good practice dictates a core set of recordable elements, however, and these are covered in this chapter. I also recommend additional elements.[1] These are not in widespread use but have proved highly valuable for me during my years as a risk practitioner. I suggest that you do not record more than you need to, however, since this will just create extra work. Think about whether particular elements will ever be needed after you have recorded them: for analysis purposes, by a programme or Project Office or by a sponsor, for example.

Table 5.5 shows a risk register that I recommend. You will see that it is divided into three layers, each separated by a horizontal double line. The top layer deals with the initial identification of a risk. The middle layer is for the assessment of the risk and the bottom layer is for the risk response.

Dividing the register in this way allows you to record only the necessary information for a risk at its relevant stage in the risk management process. Thus, on identifying a risk, only the top layer needs to be completed. There will be occasions, of course, when all three layers will be completed at once. To derive the most benefit from this register it is important to utilise all the fields over the appropriate stages of risk management.

The risk register is basically the same structure whether it be for use at the project or the programme level. At the programme level, it would be useful to include an additional field to indicate the projects affected.

The risk identification layer

Taking one of the two risks identified in Table 2.1 in Chapter 2, *Identifying and expressing risk*, we could record it in simple terms as:

Risk Number	Risk		
R1	Because of a need to add extra routing to the design	there is a risk that pipe-flow testing may be late	resulting in a delay to the project schedule.

It is helpful to maintain the three separate parts of the risk in individual compartments. This ensures that the cause, risk and effect are brought out in the overall risk statement, and is particularly useful as a guide for team members not used to expressing risk in this way.

Numbering risks enables them to be quickly identified, and is an essential component of the risk log, where brevity is all important. The risk log entry for the above might look like this:

Risk No.	Risk
R1	Risk that pipe-flow testing may be late

There are no rules for risk numbering, but I have seen many elegant interpretations of this requirement. Codes may be used for identifying the sub-project to which the risk refers or for identifying the date it was raised, for example. I quite like an arrangement for the latter, where a date is appended to a unique number. So, R1603001 is the first risk raised in March, 2016. When scanning a log this clearly shows how old the risk is, reminding people of its overdue status, perhaps.

If simplicity is your requirement, "R1" is perfectly acceptable (I recommend using the letter R in order to differentiate between a risk and any other project exceptions capable of being numbered, such as an issue (I) or a change (C)).

It is useful to be able to specify the area of the project affected by the risk and, if applicable, the sub-project name. This grouping is helpful when performing risk analysis. Risks can be charted by sub-project and/or focus area. The name of the person who identified the risk is also useful, plus the date it was raised. When a risk owner is assigned later it is helpful for that person to know who to contact for further information about the risk and the circumstances under which it was raised.

To complete our examination of the top layer (risk identification) you will find it useful to assign a status to the risk. The *Risk Status* field appears in the top layer but, in practice, it applies to all three layers, since the status codes you will assign will change according to the risk's position in the risk management process.

Table 5.1 Sample risk status codes

Code	Explanation
NEW	New risk awaiting assessment.
ASSESSED	Assessed risk awaiting response actions. (It is the risk owner's responsibility to ensure that actions and action owners are assigned.)
ACTIONED	Response actions have been assigned.
CLOSED	No longer a risk, for whatever reason.

Table 5.2 Sample risk identification layer of a risk register

Risk No.	Sub-Project	Area Affected	Raised By	Date Raised	Risk Status
R1603001	Pipe-flow design	A6 Application	Peter Simpson	04 Mar 2016	NEW

Cause	Risk	Impact
Because of a need to add extra routing to the design	there is a risk that pipe-flow testing may be late	resulting in a delay to the project schedule.

You will find it helpful to select some status codes for use with this field. Your company may have preferred codes, but I like to keep them simple and memorable and relate them to the progress of the risk through the risk management process. Table 5.1 shows my preferences.

Using the risk example in this chapter, the risk identification layer might look like that in Table 5.2.

The risk assessment layer

This layer is concerned with assessing the risk's likelihood of occurrence, its impact to the project and the cost of its impact. Risk assessment can be done at the same time as a risk is identified; though, more typically, it is done later, since it can be a more involved process and require expert input. Often, a risk owner would be assigned, usually from within the project team, whose job would be to ensure that the risk is adequately assessed. (Refer to Chapter 3, *Assessing risk*, for details of the process.)

The assessment layer includes the field *Assessment Comments*. This is useful for anyone reassessing the risk, since the comments in this field indicate why the risk has been assessed as a particular probability and impact. An example of assessment comments is given below:

Assessment Comments
Situation has occurred before (ref. XYZ project), so likely to occur again. Impact would severely affect the design stage. Impact cost includes cost of redesigning the ABC component.

The assessment layer includes some fields that may be quantified: *Probability %, Impact %, Impact Cost* and *Risk Exposure*. These fields work together and can be powerful indicators when used in conjunction with the total cost of the project. I recommend using the following order for inputting these fields:

1. Probability %
2. Impact Cost
3. Impact %
4. Risk Exposure

Some people prefer to break out the types of impact cost and differentiate between direct costs and indirect costs. In that case it is easy to specify additional fields.

The register dispenses with the highly inaccurate use of the qualitative values "High", "Medium" or "Low" for evaluating *Probability* or *Impact*. Instead, it requires an estimate of the percentage probability and impact.

1. Estimate the likelihood of the risk occurring (1–99%) and put the figure in the field *Probability %*. Note that a probability of 100% is invalid, since it effectively makes the risk an issue (see section on *Probability* in Chapter 3, *Assessing risk*).
2. Calculate the cost of the impact (for example, in terms of days lost and people resources needed to repair the damage) and enter it in the *Impact Cost* field. (Use the *Assessment Comments* field to give a description of the cost breakdown.)
3. Convert this figure to a percentage of the cost of the total project and enter this in the *Impact %* field. (Ensure that an estimate of the total cost of the project is entered in the box at the top of the register.) *Impact %* can be any figure from 0%, and can be higher than 100%, of course.
4. Calculate the *Risk Exposure* for the risk by multiplying the *Impact Cost* by its respective *Probability %*. A risk exposure for the total project may be calculated by totalling the risk exposures for each risk and placing the total in the box at the top of the risk register. Note that mitigating actions may reduce the figure considerably, after allowing for their cost (see the section *Calculating the risk exposure* in Chapter 3, *Assessing risk*). Be sure to differentiate between unmitigated and mitigated risk exposure.

You may feel that calculating the *Impact %* is superfluous. However, it is both a useful quick indicator of impact when comparing risks in the register and a useful figure for reporting purposes.

The *Risk Owner* is specified in the appropriate field. For information on assigning risk owners, see *Assigning risk owners* in Chapter 3, *Assessing risk*.

A *Time Window* field allows you to estimate the currency of the risk. When might it impact? In our example we estimate the impact could occur in approximately 2 months. This field is also known as *Proximity* in some risk registers.

The *Priority* field is available for indicating the importance of the risk. A numerical indication may be used (say, 1, 2 or 3) or a qualitative statement, such

Table 5.3 Sample risk assessment layer of a risk register

Prob. %	Impact %	Risk Owner	Time Window	Priority	Risk Exposure £K	Impact Cost £K	Assessment Comments
60	5	Simon Edwards	2 mths.	1	1.8	3.0	Two week's delay at £1.5K per week.

as high, medium or low. Clearly, the priority would reflect both the probability of the risk occurring and its severity of impact.

Our assessment layer might now look like the example shown in Table 5.3. Regarding the *Impact %*, the total project cost is £60K in this example.

The above fields probably represent the minimum most useful for assessing project risks. Some projects may require more sophisticated or company-specific measures.

The risk response layer

The risk response layer contains the fields necessary to control the assignment of actions to deal with the risk.

Each action has a separate action number. I recommend using the same format as for the numbering of the risk itself, but using the designation "A" instead of "R". Alternatively, a more simple numbering may be used, such as A1, A2, etc., or the action may be tied in with the risk, such as R1/A1 (Action 1 of Risk 1). Whatever method chosen, it is important to understand how the actions will be monitored and controlled on a regular basis. It is possible, for example, to control the actions from all the project exceptions together (risks, issues and changes), in which case a suitable identification for each would be required.

The risk response layer also includes fields for estimating the reduction in probability and impact, since it is reasonable to assume that the probability and impact might be reduced as a result of performing some actions. If an action does not reduce one or both of these the risk owner must question whether the action is worthwhile, since performing any action costs time as well as money. However, some zero reduction actions are necessary as preparation for a follow-on action.

The *Priority* field is useful for highlighting which actions should be worked on first. Thus, priority 1 actions would take precedent over priority 2 actions. The amount of probability and impact reduced by completion of an action would have an effect on deciding its priority.

The *Cost* field is for capturing the cost of the action. It is particularly necessary for *contingency* actions, i.e., actions that involve putting something in place in case the risk impacts. (Refer to Action A0203003 in Table 5.4.)

The *Action Owner* field is for specifying the person who will take responsibility for ensuring that an action is carried out. Note that this is not necessarily

Table 5.4 Sample risk response layer of a risk register

Action No.	Response Action	Action Owner	Priority	Due Date	Reduction in Prob. %	Reduction in Impact %	Cost £K	Action Status
A1603001	Clarify the need to add extra routing. How certain is the requirement?	Mary Brown	1	01/04/2016				01/04/2016. Closed. Requirement not certain. Suggest specialist view.
A1603002	Perform a detailed assessment of the pipe-flow test plan and identify slack in the schedule.	Mary Brown	1	01/04/2016		–2%		01/04/2016. Closed. Schedule could be reduced by 3/4 days.
A1603003	Devise contingency plan for outsourcing the ABC design work.	Karen Johnson	2	29/04/2016	–40%		1K	

the person who will undertake the action. A group of persons may be required to undertake the action, but it is important to have one person accountable for seeing it through.

Finally, the *Action Status* field is a useful record of progress against an action. The project manager or Project Office can use this field to record items from say, a weekly status meeting.

Our sample risk might now look like that of the response layer in Table 5.4.

The full register entry for this risk now looks like that in Table 5.5. Table A.1 in Appendix A shows a full blank register.

The risk log

The risk log is essentially a one-line summary of each risk in the risk register. As such, it is a very useful aid, for example, at weekly progress meetings. Only essential detail is captured, and the choice of what is essential is down to the individual project. If the risk register is automated, then the risk log can be generated automatically. Table 5.6 gives an example.

If the risk log is to be of value it needs to be unambiguous. Logs containing a risk number but no description of the risks will be difficult to use, unless everyone has a very good memory!

Mechanising the register

It is perfectly possible to use a paper-based risk register and log for a small, contained project, but for a larger project it is better to use a computer application. This could be something constructed specially for use as a company standard or it could be an application purchased "off the shelf".

Before deciding how to do this, it is worth considering its use and purpose. The register is primarily a vehicle for control. The ability to undertake analysis and produce reports is more important than purely recording the data. I have seen many home-grown registers that have been excellent recording vehicles but have fallen remarkably short on analysis and reporting. In programming terms, these latter tend to be more problematic and time-consuming to construct, so are often poorly contrived.

In a large project it is likely that a Project Office will maintain the risk register, entering data and producing regular reports. Access might be granted to individuals, such as risk owners, so that progress on their risks can be updated directly. In this case, it might be beneficial to have a web-based application, which would facilitate easy access from almost anywhere in the world. An interactive application would enable information to be sent to action owners and risk owners, such as reminders of overdue actions or completion of actions.

For me, an ideal application is one that incorporates risks, issues and changes all in one database. Unfortunately, I know of none that exist off the shelf, though I have constructed them myself for particular projects. However, such an application would cater for the common element of all these project exceptions – actions.

Table 5.5 Sample risk register, incorporating all three layers with worked example

Risk No.	Sub-Project	Area Affected	Raised By	Date Raised	Risk Status
R1603001	Systems Design	A6 Application	Peter Simpson	04 Mar 2016	ACTIONED

Cause		Risk		Impact	
Because of a need to add extra routing to the pipework design		there is a risk that pipe-flow testing may be late		resulting in a delay to the project schedule.	

Prob. %	Impact %	Risk Owner	Time Window	Priority	Risk Exposure £K	Impact Cost £K	Assessment Comments
60	5	Simon Edwards	2 mths.	1	1.8	3.0	Two week's delay at £1.5K per week.

Action No.	Response Action	Action Owner	Priority	Due Date	Reduction in Prob. %	Reduction in Impact %	Cost £K	Action Status
A160 3001	Clarify the need to add extra routing. How certain is the requirement?	Mary Brown	1	01/04/2016				01/04/2016. Closed. Requirement not certain. Suggest specialist view.
A160 3002	Perform a detailed assessment of the pipe-flow test plan and identify slack in the schedule.	Mary Brown	1	01/04/2016		−2%		01/04/2016. Initial assessment reveals that schedule could be reduced by 3/4 days.
A160 3003	Devise contingency plan for outsourcing the ABC design work.	Karen Johnson	2	29/04/2016	−40%		1K	

Table 5.6 Example of entries in a risk log

Risk No.	Sub-Project	Risk Summary	Date Raised	Risk Status	Risk Owner	Prob. %	Impact %	RE £K	Comments
R1601001	Bus. Analysis	risk that the business owners will not have time for actions	1-Jan-02	ACTIONED	ASD	60%	8%	8.40	
R1601002	Bus. Analysis	risk that data will not be available when needed	1-Jan-02	ACTIONED	ASD	30%	1%	0.60	
R1601003	Communication	risk that show home availability will be delayed	3-Jan-02	ACTIONED	TP	40%	1%	1.20	
R1601004	Communication	risk that marketing will not be ready before the holiday period	3-Jan-02	CLOSED	TP	30%	6%	6.00	Risk avoided 24.01
R1602001	Insulation Test	risk that test equipment will not be ready	3-Feb-02	ACTIONED	LM	60%	6%	6.00	
R1602002	Production	risk of poor quality of roof trusses from fabricator	12-Feb-02	ASSESSED	BN	25%	2%	2.00	
R1602003	Production	risk of build failure in G type components	23-Feb-02	NEW	JJB				

It would also enable a risk to be viewed in context and not as a stand–alone element. The pathway of risks to issues and changes has already been described in the *Introduction* of this book.

Figures 5.1, 5.2 and 5.3 show sample pages from a purpose-built risk register, coded using SQL. The screens are fairly simple in design. As already stated, the complexity is not in the data input, but rather the analysis and reporting.

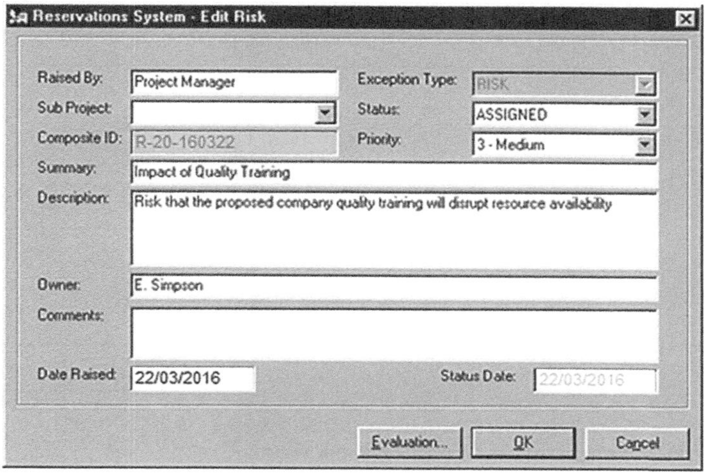

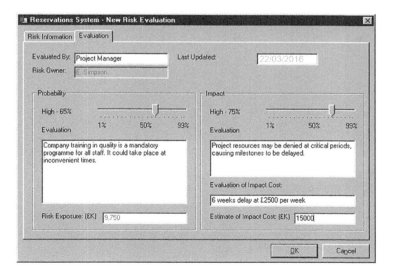

Figure 5.1 Identification page from a purpose-built risk register

Figure 5.2 Assessment page from a purpose-built risk register

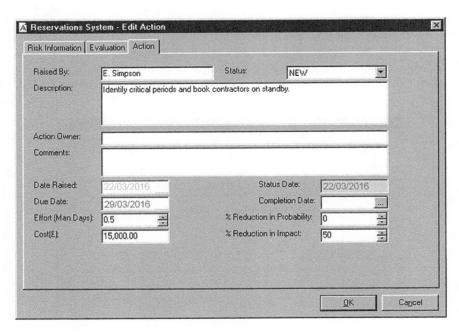

Figure 5.3 Actions page from a purpose-built risk register

Note

1 (NB. Detailed explanations of each risk element are given in the chapters to which they refer.)

6   Analysing and reporting risk

Risk analysis is the use of risk data to create information that will help make decisions about the project. The information may be in the form of charts, models, lists or reports. A significant amount of data may be accumulated in a project – even more in a programme. A fully completed risk register, for example, can hold a lot of data and there are many ways that this data can be used to provide useful information. This chapter shows a few that I have found useful for particular purposes.

Risk modelling

One of the best ways of analysing risk is to construct a model of risk for your programme or project. There are various methods of modelling risk, but I prefer to use a technique that I call risk concept mapping. It is effectively a team's concept of the things that could cause risk (the risk drivers), the situations in which risk may present itself (the risk situations) and the possible impacts. Risk concept mapping utilises Soft Systems Methodology, a concept pioneered by Lancaster University in the 1980s.

For those accustomed only to a risk register, a risk concept map may not seem to have a direct correlation. This is deliberate. The concepts of risk drivers, situations and impacts do not directly equate to typical risk register entries of cause, risk event and impact. The exception is impact, which most will recognise as being similar to that recorded in a risk register. The reason there is no direct correlation is that the risk concept map is designed to be a step taken before the construction of risk statements that would appear in a risk register. The risk concept map provides an overall background from which it will be easier to formulate risk statements than from a mere brainstorming exercise.

Risk concept mapping

The benefit of this technique is that, for only few hours' work, a team can have a picture of the worst-case risk that may be encountered during the life of a project or programme, and the events that may lead to it. The resultant map shows pathways from risk drivers to risk situations and risk outcomes. It also shows risk increasing in impact towards a final outcome. Because the input to the map is derived from teamwork, its ownership is quickly assured, thus making it easier to plan responses to the risk.

The technique is useful at any stage of a project, but can be commenced well before project start-up. It is particularly powerful at any pre-project bidding stage when a company needs to know the full picture of risk before making a proposal.

Figure 6.1 shows a high-level risk concept map of possible risk drivers leading to increasing degrees of risk situations and impacts. The risk drivers (squares) are not risks themselves but are possible environments or trigger points for risk. They trigger risk situations (circles, light shade) that give rise to firstly risk situations then to risk impacts (circles, dark shade). The risk situations are similar to risk drivers in that they are also not themselves risks, except that they describe events or situations that could be triggered by the risk drivers. Many risks could result from a single risk situation. The impacts tend to increase in severity towards a final, worst-case impact. I find that the looseness of structure around drivers and situations helps to build a breeding ground for the more formal risk statements (cause, risk event, impact) that will eventually populate a risk register. In this example you will notice that most of the mapped information is conceptual, i.e., not physical elements. The physical elements are more likely to occur at a lower level, where the detail starts to emerge. So, for example, if you were to examine the impact "Some work is missed", you would very likely reveal the specific nature of the work missed. Constructing the map using an appropriate software drawing application might allow you to click on a high-level object and reveal a lower-level map.

The map reads from left to right and is best constructed in a group session. Although it is best to commence with the risk drivers, the symbols do not have to be rigidly built-up in order. It is normal, for example, for the team to think of some worst-case impacts before some of the risk situations have been identified. In this case, the impacts can be placed to right of the map, ready for the pathways leading to them to be defined.

The map represents the team's assumptions of the events that could occur in an unconstrained environment. Several iterations may be needed before the map is deemed complete by the project team. The map tends to become stable quite quickly, the risk situations and impacts requiring little alteration over time, thus giving the team confidence in knowing the potential risk they may encounter.

It is possible to relate resulting individual risks to the risk situations. Figure 6.2 shows how this can be done graphically. This more detailed map shows risk numbers (small circles) which relate to entries in a risk register. Adding individual risks means that the map will need regular updating, however. A benefit is that it is able to show the risks in context. Immediately, it is possible to see which risk situations are associated with several risk statements and which risk situations are associated with very few or none. It is also feasible to add the probabilities to the impacts, and an average could be calculated for all the risks along each pathway.

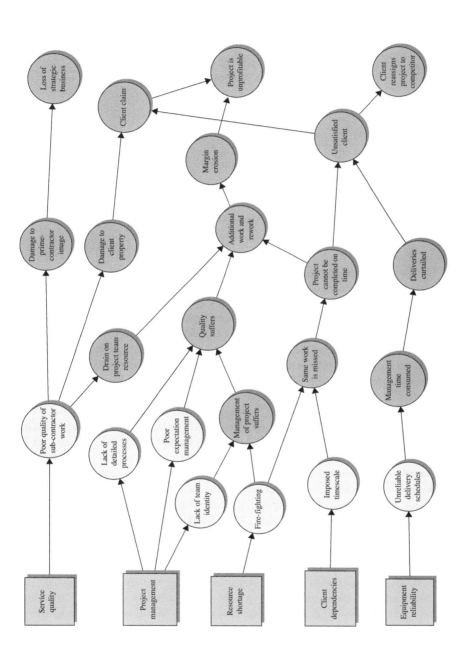

Figure 6.1 Example of a simple high-level risk concept map relating to building refurbishment work for a client

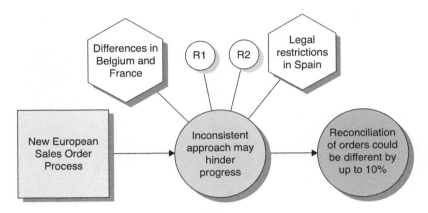

Figure 6.2 Example of a risk pathway using the full symbol set

The risk concept map in Figure 6.2 is based on one of the maps constructed in support of a programme to cater for the changeover of local country currency to the Euro. You will notice that it shows hexagons in addition to the symbol set used in Figure 6.1. These represent assumptions about the risk situations and are a useful way of providing supporting information. Assumptions, in this context, are a general use of the word and can be used in several ways. They can aid risk assessment, since they can state an opinion at the time the map is created that can be validated over time. They can clarify the text in the squares or circles or enhance the argument, as in the assumption *"volume testing cannot fully simulate use over time"* for the risk situation *"robustness of notes and coins over time has yet to be proven"*. They can point to specific instances of a risk situation or impact, as in *"local practice"* for the risk situation *"different approaches to hardware, software, etc."*. They can suggest a response for a risk situation, as in *"banks need to consider staff incentives"* for the situation *"retention of required resources may be difficult and costly"*.

By showing risk in a flow diagram format, some interesting aspects are revealed. Firstly, there is the aspect of clustering. In Figure 6.3, the impacts *"potential for widespread system crashes"*, *"potential for help desk call surge"* and *"bank customer dissatisfaction"* appear as key nodes, since more than one risk situation contributes to each. Many impacts have more than one cause, so clustering helps to identify graphically the causal contributions.

Secondly, risk pathways may be identified. Figure 6.3 shows a minimal risk pathway using the full symbol set. Where these pathways contribute to other pathways is significant. A stand-alone risk register would not be able to show this easily.

Risk concept maps may be nested. An overall map could represent the risk for an entire programme and lower-level maps could be constructed for individual projects.

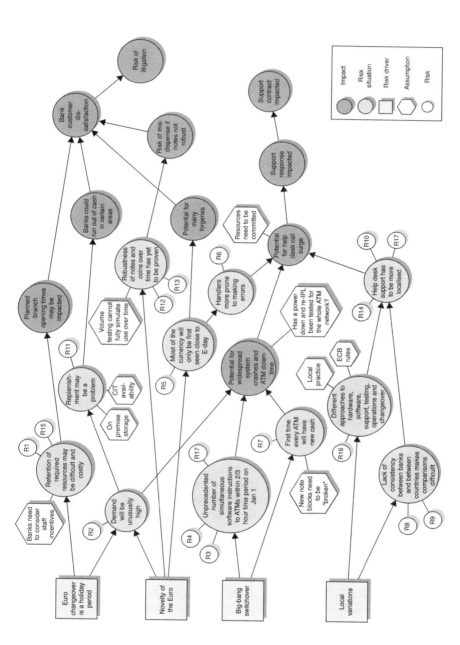

Figure 6.3 Example of a risk concept map for a Euro changeover project for automated teller machines (ATM) (courtesy NCR Ltd.)

Used in conjunction with cause-and-effect diagrams, risk concept maps can be a useful means of showing the overall risk picture for a project or programme.

Cause-and-effect diagrams

Cause-and-effect diagrams (also known as Ishikawa diagrams) show contributors (causes) to a single outcome (impact), whereas the risk concept map can display multiple outcomes. However, the cause-and-effect diagram is a good vehicle for displaying more detail than a risk concept map. It is useful, for example, for showing additional detail for risk pathways leading to a single impact on a risk concept map. Figure 6.4 demonstrates this for the risk pathways from Figure 6.3 that lead to the impact *"bank customer dissatisfaction"*.

Cause-and-effect diagrams are also useful for investigating a problem that has occurred, since they can be constructed retrospectively, extrapolating back to the causes of the problem. This is helpful during project close-out when attempting to learn lessons from the project. However, why wait for an impact to happen? Use a cause-and-effect diagram to model *"what ifs?"* For example, if you have a strong concern that a key component may be delivered late from a supplier, you could construct a cause-and-effect diagram with your team to try to understand why the component may be late, and so be able to prevent it from happening. See Figure 8.4 in Chapter 8, *Managing risk*, for an example.

Infinite branches may be constructed for each contributing concept, allowing a very fine level of granularity. It is difficult, however, to show interdependencies across the branches. The risk concept map is able to do this well, subject to having too many lines crossing, and so cluttering the map.

The cause-and-effect diagram displays clusters of contributions well. Figure 6.4 shows that "Dispensing accuracy" can be shown as a discrete series of branches, as well as "High demand". This enables the viewer to focus easily on all the causes relating to a single aspect.

Variants of the cause-and-effect diagram described above exist in some industries. These may show the effect as an impact, centrally focussed, with a network of causes leading to it from one side and a network of recovery actions leading to it from the other. Similarly, in safety risk practice, this might be an incident as the central focus, with causes and consequences contributing to it.

Cause-and-effect diagrams are particularly useful in risk identification. They can act as a fast path to identifying the first part of a risk statement: the causes.

To construct a cause-and-effect diagram, first state the event with which you are concerned to the right of a large white board. In Figure 6.4 this is "Customer dissatisfaction". Next draw a single line across the board leading to this event. This is the spine of the diagram. Select some categories to focus on and place these either side of the spine. In Figure 6.4 there are only two categories: "Dispensing accuracy" and "High demand". Keep your categories high level, since the detail will be contained within the body of the diagram. A typical diagram may contain four to six categories, placed either side of the spine. For

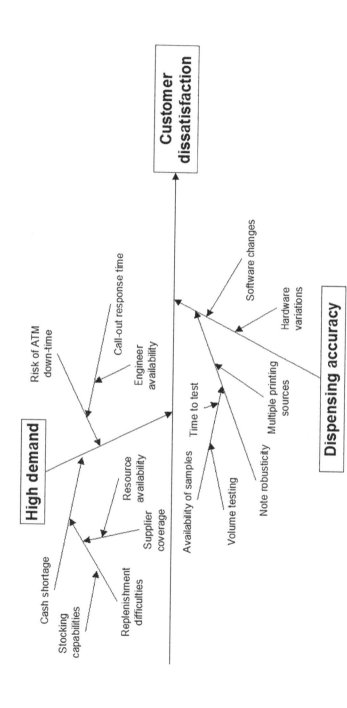

Figure 6.4 A single impact from Figure 6.3 expressed as a cause-and-effect diagram

example, "Communication", "Suppliers", "Technical" and "Client" are good general categories. Connect each category to the spine along a diagonal axis.

It is important to construct the diagram with a team of people, in order to achieve a reasonable consensus. To get to the first level down from each category, ask the question "Why?" For example, "Why might there be supplier problems?" The team should be able to identify some areas for concern that can be placed as off-shoots to the "Supplier" axis. Asking "Why?" at each level enables the team to drill down to deeper causes. It is usually not necessary to go lower than three levels in a typical project situation, but in some cases it may be worth trying to reach the root cause of a problem.

It is quite valid to have the same cause appear on different category axes. "Lack of funding", for example, could appear more than once. This would indicate the importance of this cause to the whole problem.

Once you have reached what you believe to be *root causes*, you have the opportunity to propose some solutions. By asking "How?" from the lowest level to the top, you are able to state how you can avoid the potential risks. Figure 6.5 shows this concept. Thus, the Ishikawa diagram can not only identify causes but also aid with responses to risks.

Influence diagrams and decision trees

Influence diagrams and decision trees are similar types of diagram that show the effect of decisions in relation to chance events. These decisions may be quantified and may lead to one or more numerical outcomes, such as cost, revenue or profit. Several software applications exist to assist the construction of influence diagrams and decision trees.

The influence diagram may have some similarities to the risk concept map in appearance, but it is more aligned to a decision tree in concept, though the decision tree tends to be more structured than the freer-format influence diagram.

Whereas the risk concept map models the extent of risk towards ultimate impacts, the influence diagram is able to model how to deal with a risk situation. A diagrammatical difference between a risk concept map and an influence diagram is that the nodes of the influence diagram represent events and decisions rather than situations and impacts.

Figure 6.5 Schematic of questions to generate causes and responses

The influence diagram is useful for indicating possible scenarios for responding to one or more risks. There do not seem to be any official rules for constructing it, though some software packages adopt a particular format. I like to use the format shown in the example in Figure 6.6. This example shows three possible decision pathways from a risk event and the relative cost of the decisions towards an ultimate value (pentagons). Each decision (square) is followed by events (circles) that influence the next decision.

Figure 6.7 shows the symbol set I like to use, though there is no standard. Figure 6.7 ably depicts the various options for dealing with a particular risk event. A decision tree could show the same options and has the ability to show more detail. So, which is the best diagram to use? Often both are used, but for different purposes. The influence diagram can be a better visual representation of the high-level data, whereas the decision tree can be the supporting statistical evidence. A decision tree also follows a strict chronological order.

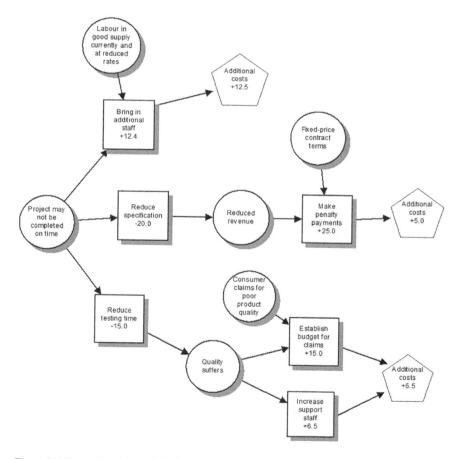

Figure 6.6 Example of a simple influence diagram

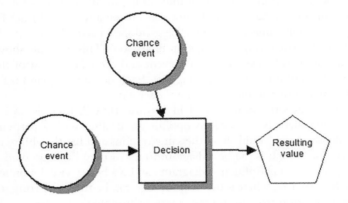

Figure 6.7 Symbol set for an influence diagram

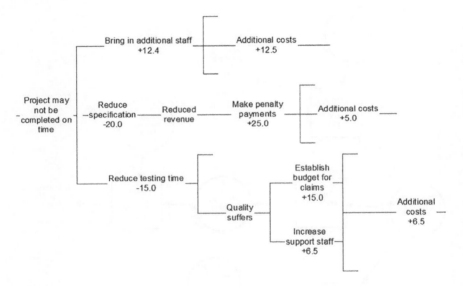

Figure 6.8 Decision tree version of Figure 6.6

Figure 6.8 shows the same data as Figure 6.6, but in the decision tree structure. Figure 6.9 shows a more complex decision tree. Though this example is not quantified, it demonstrates the use of a decision tree for making and testing assumptions. The results of decisions are often two-fold: negative or positive (yes or no).

Decision tree data can be presented in different formats. It can be summarised to good effect, as in Figure 6.10, where the detailed tree structure might detract from the key points being made. It shows the risk exposures calculated for a new

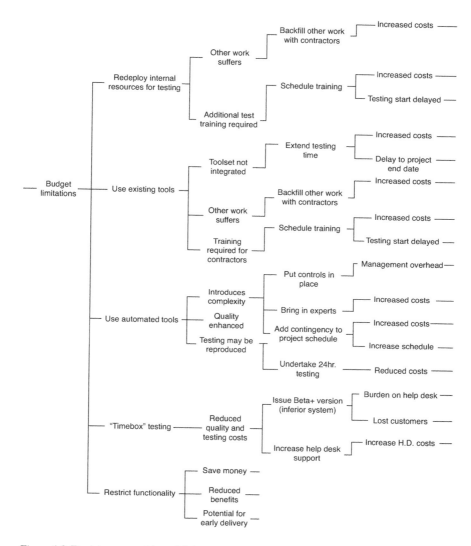

Figure 6.9 Decision tree with multiple options

mobile phone product, and the choice between launching the product early to achieve competitive edge or delaying launch until further testing had been carried out. The pressures by the business on the project team for the early launch option were considerable, but the result shows the latter option carried the least risk, even though the margin of error in calculating the risk exposures was great. Only the summary risk factors are shown for each option.

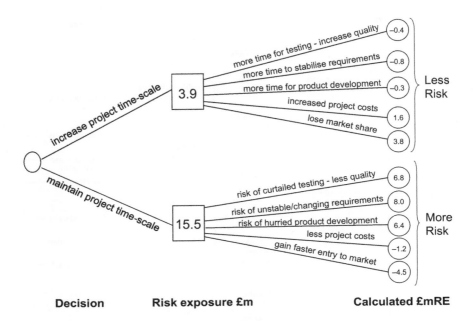

Decision	Risk exposure £m	Calculated £mRE

Figure 6.10 Chart showing decision tree data for deciding best of two options

Monte Carlo simulation

Monte Carlo simulation is a form of risk modelling that focuses on the likelihood of scheduled dates or budgets being met. It may be constructed manually, but this can be quite time-consuming, and, today, most charts are constructed using specialist software, either embedded in a planning tool or as a stand-alone application.

A range of possibilities is examined by running several hundred samplings (often known as iterations) of every possible value or outcome to produce a graph showing either the most likely range of costs and the likelihood of completing the project within budget or the most likely duration for the project or projects within a programme.

Probability distributions are used in the calculation, together with any weighted values that a user inputs. The sampling performed relates to the shape of the probability distribution. The distributions have predefined shapes, such as "triangular", "normal" and "skewed". A different result is obtained through both running a different number of iterations and the action of the software's random number generator. The larger the sample, the longer the processing and the finer the result. Thus, several thousand iterations should yield a finer result than several hundred. A typical outcome of a simulation is shown in Figure 6.11. Note the skewed distribution.

The Monte Carlo technique simulates a project many times over. This would be extremely difficult for anyone to do manually, so the reliance on software is

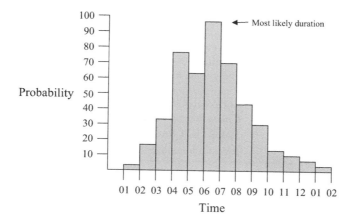

Figure 6.11 Example of output of a Monte Carlo schedule simulation (skewed distribution)

essential. Using Monte Carlo software it is possible to perform *"what if?"* scenarios, altering the input data to cater for different situations.

Reporting risk

Reporting considerations

Many project managers forget that the real reason for identifying and dealing with risk is to enable decision-making. Most project decisions should be made on a basis of risk. Therefore, the way in which risk is reported becomes particularly important. Strange then, that risk reporting is not always given the attention it deserves.

In my career I have seen, on the one hand, project reports crammed with pretty risk charts and diagrams, and, on the other hand, reports showing merely a list of risks, none of which enable constructive decision-making. I am not against pretty diagrams, as you can see from the charts in this book, but they do need to be able to convey information upon which decisions can be easily made.

As with all project reporting, it is important to know who is going to use it and what the recipient of the report is expected to do with it. It might be a project sponsor requiring monthly information in order to have advanced warning of potential problems for the business. It might be a project manager requiring weekly information on the likelihood of milestones being met. Whatever the purpose, it is important to produce reports that will be effective. In this section I show some reporting formats that can be useful for particular recipients.

Reporting should be decided prior to project start-up when the project management process is established. The opportunity to include risk reporting within the standard project reporting structure should be taken. I find it

Table 6.1 Risk reporting requirements and possible vehicles

Requirement	Possible Reporting Vehicles
Establish confidence	Chart of the number of risks by project stage, month on month. Success rate in number of risks not converted to issues.
Reduce risks	Chart showing decrease in both probabilities and number of risks, month on month.
Reduce impact	Chart showing decrease in impact costs, month on month.
Reduce risk exposure	Risk Radar Chart used comparatively.
Highlight risk severity	Risk Ribbon Chart with graduated alert status.

beneficial to include risk as part of the general reporting process, rather than as something special and stand-alone. Deciding what to report is an important part of the risk management process. A wealth of data will be collected and recorded in the risk register, and it is wise to make use of that data through analysis and reporting. The risk log, described in Chapter 5, *Recording risk*, makes a good basis for reporting data. It can be used either in its own right as a good summary of individual risks or as selected fields to accompany risk charts. Table 6.1 gives some indication of the aspects to consider and some possible means of reporting them.

Establishing confidence is an important requirement of risk management. Project sponsors, clients and, in fact, the whole team want to be assured of the successful outcome of a project. The initial risk exposure calculated at project outset may look daunting, but all parties have a vested interest in ensuring that it does not become a reality. Demonstrating confidence may be done through careful reporting. This means showing how the quantity of risks is being reduced for each project stage, week on week or month on month.

A key target is the prevention of issues. This is another demonstration of confidence. A way of measuring how effectively risk identification is being practised is to track the number of issues being raised that could have been foreseen as risks. Other metrics relating to the practice of the risk management process may be tracked, such as the time taken for risks to be assessed or actioned. Speed of process is particularly relevant for risk management.

As important as the reduction in the number of risks is a decrease in probability and impact. Some risks may never be eliminated, but a decrease in either probability or impact is just as desirable. This affects the overall risk exposure and, of course, the total cost of the project.

Overall severity (the combination of probability and impact) is a measure that many teams like to report. I find it useful to combine it with an alert status, the categories of which need to be agreed beforehand. It can be helpful in prioritising, especially for projects or programmes where the quantity of risks is great. Here, risks with a project or business critical severity are tackled first.

Examples of risk charts

The following are charts I prefer to use at various stages in the risk management process.

Risk Radar Charts

The Risk Radar Chart is a format I like to use in order to give a steering committee a quick feel for the amount of risk exposure in particular areas. The number of areas on which to focus depends on the nature of the project, but it can be useful to start with those described in the section *Identifying risk* in Chapter 2, *Identifying and expressing risk*. Tables 2.2 and 2.3 give examples. Figure 6.12 shows a simple Risk Radar Chart. The chart can be compiled using good charting or spreadsheet software.

This type of chart is highly useful for busy executives with a 10-second attention span. It is particularly effective when used in comparison, month on month. I use it mainly for charting risk exposure data, but other parameters may also be used.

Figure 6.12 is a Risk Radar Chart with the focus areas aligned to the spokes. A variant is that shown in Figure 6.13, where the focus areas are aligned to the spaces in between the spokes. In this respect, it is actually a Spider Chart, and, because it produces a more dramatic effect, it is useful where a particular point needs to be made.

Risk Ribbon Charts

The Risk Ribbon Chart is a novel way of representing more data and showing its comparison more visually than a standard bar chart. Figure 6.14 shows an example. Like the Risk Radar Chart, the Ribbon Chart may be constructed using good charting and spreadsheet software. In the example in Figure 6.14,

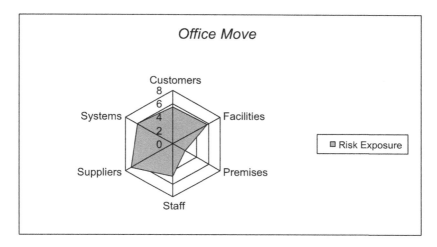

Figure 6.12 Example of a Risk Radar Chart

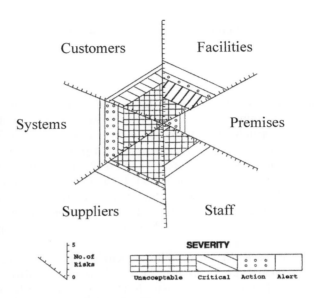

Figure 6.13 Variation on the Risk Radar Chart

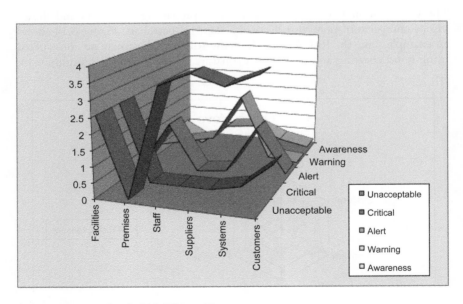

Figure 6.14 Example of a Risk Ribbon Chart

I show the effect of adding a graduated warning key, so that an audience may see instantly which areas are giving cause for concern. It is a nice chart to include in a reporting package for a project manager. The example shows the number of risks in each area, but other measures such as risk exposure may be shown, of course.

Also, like the Risk Radar Chart, it is beneficial when used in comparison on a regular basis.

Bar charts

Bar charts are useful for showing data quickly and easily. Figures 6.15 and 6.16 show their use in depicting the quantity of risks at key project stages. As you might expect, at contract award, the number of risks identified is high in the early stages (Figure 6.15). As work progresses to the build stage, the emphasis shifts (Figure 6.16). Different patterns emerge from different types of projects, of

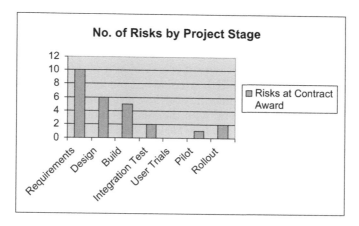

Figure 6.15 Risks by project stage – 1

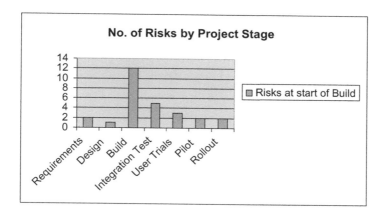

Figure 6.16 Risks by project stage – 2

course. The relative height of the bars is a good visual indicator of current status and the simplicity of this type of chart makes it useful for a variety of purposes.

Probability/Impact Matrix

This type of chart is a matrix of probability against impact cost and has some use in establishing the priority of risks during risk assessment, in order to assign actions. The matrix is best constructed using a measure of qualification, such as *Very High*, *High*, *Medium*, *Low* and *Very Low*. You will need to convert your percentages of probability to the relevant categories. This can either be a straight apportionment or skewed for those, for example, who rate any probability above 40% as high. (See the section *Probability* in Chapter 3, *Assessing risk*.)

There are various permutations possible using this matrix, depending on what you want to emphasise. Some people use additional input, which, combined with the probability and impact data, emphasises things such as severity, urgency or cost. Weightings and rankings can also be applied. I prefer to show just the risk exposure. Choose the method that helps you prioritise best the risks. Figure 6.17 shows an example of the matrix that displays risk exposures in the grid squares.

Warning: A danger with this type of chart is that it prompts you to concentrate on the higher quadrants, and there could be a tendency to ignore those risks in the lower quadrants. Sometimes it is the low probability risks that can cause the most disruption, so be careful with the interpretation. Figure 6.17 shows a large concentration of risk in the *Very High* impact box but *Very Low* in terms of probability. It would be foolish to ignore this.

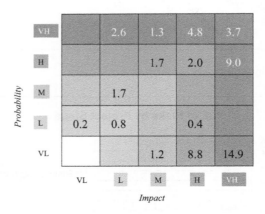

Figure 6.17 Example of a Probability/Impact Matrix

7 Administering risk

The risk management process

The ongoing management of risk should be based around a documented process. This is so that everyone in the team knows what is expected of him or her in terms of risk identification, assessment, response, reporting, analysis and control. Most project management methodologies incorporate some form of risk management process and some specify tools and techniques to be used. The exact procedure to follow, therefore, may be dictated either by a preferred project or programme management methodology or by company standards. Appendix A gives a sample, which you are free to adopt or adapt, as required.

The process of risk management may be divided into discrete cycles, as shown in Figure 7.1. There are differing views regarding the terminology, even though there has been much agreement of terminology throughout Europe and the USA during recent years. Certainly, there is no disagreement regarding the cyclical nature of risk management.

Each of the stages is covered within a separate chapter in this book. However, some general comments are needed regarding the overall management of risk.

Too often, I have seen risks identified at project outset, but no new risks identified. This practice suggests that both the project and the business environments remain static during the life of the project, which is, of course, just not true. When I audit projects I expect to see a risk register larger than the project issues log. This tells me that new risks are being regularly identified and being prevented from becoming issues by the ongoing practice of good risk management.

In the same way that new risks ought to be regularly identified, so existing risks should be regularly reassessed. As work progresses and becomes familiar the existing estimates of probability and impact are bound to change. A good opportunity to reassess risks, of course, comes when response actions are completed. Their completion should reduce either or both the probability and impact of the risks to which they relate.

Communication is vital for successful risk management, so the risk management process needs to specify who communicates what to whom, how, why and when. Risks need to be visible to the whole project team. The use of a web-enabled tool is ideal for displaying the up-to-the-minute status of risks or for

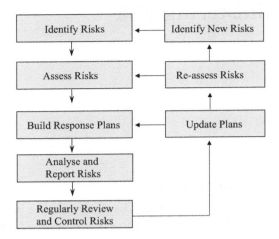

Figure 7.1 Risk management cycles

capturing information from members of the team. Too many projects allow no involvement from the team in updating risks, leaving it to a single member of the Project Office to be in control of the data. Certainly, the risk register needs to be owned by a single person, but inviting input from the team is an important aid to them buying into the process.

The regular involvement of the team can also be brought about through progress reporting. Having risks on the agenda of weekly status meetings, for example, maintains the regular contact between Project Office project manager and the team. Weekly status meetings are useful checkpoints for risk, as well as other project exceptions, such as issues and changes.

Risk roles

Every team member has a role to play in managing risk, and when I say "team", I mean the core members plus contributing parties (sub-contractors, sponsors, etc.). I have already mentioned the specific roles of risk owner and action owner, which I describe in more detail below.

There is also the more formal role of risk manager. It is a role more commonly found in a programme, but major project undertakings, particularly those that are safety critical, will probably also employ this role. As I stated in the introduction to this book, I feel that project managers do not generally make good risk managers, so the employment of a specialist risk manager is sometimes necessary. The risk management techniques described in this book are appropriate for general project and programme use, but more sophisticated techniques would be required for particular undertakings. It is appropriate to consider the techniques in this book as a good basis for building any additional requirements needed. A good risk manager would be able to build these requirements.

Risk owners

Some aspects of the risk owner role are given in the section *Assigning risk owners* in Chapter 3, *Assessing risk*, and in Chapter 4, *Responding to risk*. Further details are given here.

The role of the risk owner is to ensure that a risk is properly assessed and responded to. It is a transient role and can be undertaken by any member of the project team. It is likely in a large project that several members of the project team will act as risk owners during any one period. However, risk owners need to be people with the necessary expertise for owning the risks, since they need to be able to recommend action plans. A risk owner's expertise should be able to identify what actions might be appropriate and who should carry them out, either from direct knowledge or from seeking out those who have the right knowledge. The project manager would make the decision whether it is feasible for the actions to be carried out.

The role requires diplomacy as well as knowledge. Persuading people to act as action owners will inevitably result in close negotiations, and the project manager will probably need to add weight to the argument.

At project status meetings, the risk owners should give an update on the assignment of actions and recommend any change to the risk assessment. Monitoring the progress of actions can be delegated to the Project Office, but the interpretation and evaluation of the actions will most likely be done by the risk owners.

Action owners

The risk owners should have a responsibility to ensure that actions are specified for the risks they own. They should also ensure that each action for their risks has an action owner assigned. This may be themselves, depending on the nature of the action, though frequently it is somebody else.

An action owner does not need to be connected directly to a project, so a risk owner must ensure that any action owners assigned outside of a project agree to perform the actions. Action owners may not necessarily carry out the actions themselves, but they should ensure that the most appropriate person does. A departmental head, for example, might be assigned as an action owner, but the action might be carried out by one or more members of the department.

Action owners are responsible for reporting back progress on each action to the risk owners. This ensures not only that someone is accountable for each action, but also prevents actions from being forgotten. It will be necessary to enter certain actions as tasks in the project plan, as the effort in performing them will affect the schedule, the cost base and, possibly, resource demand and allocation.

As actions are completed, risk owners should be able to recommend the reassessment of their risks, suitably changing the probability and impact.

The risk manager

The appointment of an experienced risk manager ensures that risk is taken seriously and that it has a professional focus. Particular projects would benefit from this and could justify the overhead. Also, programmes, with their close alignment to a business strategy and their potential to deliver large-scale change, would benefit from this role.

A risk manager would establish the risk management process and give guidance to individual projects and sub-projects in their identification, assessment and management of risk, offering to facilitate risk identification and assessment workshops and ensuring consistency in the risk management process.

A risk manager must also be able to engage expertise in the identification and assessment of risk and to take a balanced view of its management. Expertise may be drawn from within a project or programme, within the company or externally, and a risk manager would probably be the person who would assign risk owners.

A risk manager would also ensure that risks are analysed to defined levels of quality and would decide whether qualitative or quantitative analysis techniques should be used.

The role can be complex and taxing. In a technical programme, the risk manager may be dealing with life-threatening possibilities. A risk manager is usually able to see the "big picture" and make an overall judgement of the various interdependencies.

Project Office

A project administrator is an ideal person to manage the risk register. Either working individually or as part of a Project Office team, he or she would administer the data in the register, ensuring that it is up-to-date. Various reports would need to be prepared using the data in the register as a basis. (See the section *Reporting risk* in Chapter 6, *Analysing and reporting risk*.)

Figure 7.2 shows the risk management cycle (dark shaded boxes) together with the main Project Office risk inputs (light shaded boxes). Essential activities by the Project Office during the cycle include the monitoring of progress against actions and the chasing of risk owners and action owners for assessment and action information.

The provision of trigger information (whether automatic or manual) is particularly important for risk owners, and the Project Office needs to ensure that the process does not lag. This can easily happen if information is not forthcoming for a period of time. All team members will have other things to do besides risk management, so need regular reminders. A fully automated system can be of benefit, using due dates and calculating optimal time intervals for each stage of the process, but it is no real substitute for the human touch.

The project manager

If there is no risk manager appointed, the project manager would take on some of the responsibilities of the risk manager role. Many project managers understand risk, but are not usually professionally trained risk managers. However, the project manager needs to own the risk management process and be accountable for identifying and managing the risk for his or her project.

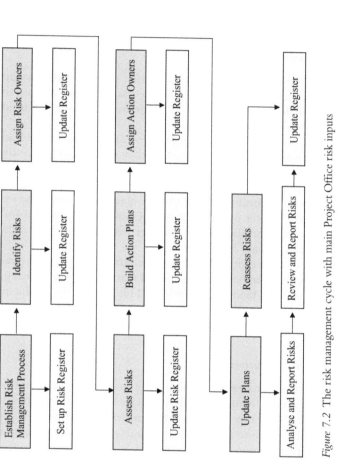

Figure 7.2 The risk management cycle with main Project Office risk inputs

In some ways, there is a conflicting mindset between that of risk manager and that of project manager. The risk manager needs to be a lateral thinker, seeing beyond a particular activity by placing it in its business context. The project manager wants to see the bottom line and be assured that schedule, cost and quality will be met.

The project manager will require regular reporting of risk in order to make controlling decisions. Likewise, the project manager will need to make reports to the project sponsor and board, requesting action on exceptional situations.

The project sponsor and board

The project sponsor and board have a key role to play in the management of risk. They will be interested in the overall risk exposure against the budget apportioned for the project. Similarly, a programme sponsor will need to know this for each project within a programme.

A sponsor or board will also need to approve exceptional expenditure for risk action or contingency plans. In doing this, they need to weigh up the amount of risk they are prepared to accept and the cost and effect of risk reduction or avoidance against the severity of the impacts. They may also need to contribute to and approve opportunities arising from risk assessments (see the section *Risk as opportunity* in Chapter 8, *Managing risk*). Good data is essential for this type of decision-making, and the project manager needs to ensure that the relevant research and analyses have been made.

The decisions will be more difficult at the programme level. In programmes, the focus on risk in the business environment and marketplace usually has greater significance than at the individual project level. This is partly due to the importance a programme holds within an overall business strategy, but also to the vulnerability of a programme in today's rapidly changing markets and business priorities.

Suppliers and sub-contractors

In a large project or programme where there may be suppliers and consultants working either internally or externally, it will be important for the project manager to encourage their buy-in to the risk management process. The provision of facilities to enable them to input risks is desirable. They may already input risks in their own organisations in a different format, so the project manager should persuade them to adopt the project standard for their work on the project. The Project Office would not want to spend time trying to convert files and data to match the project's systems.

Monitoring and controlling risks

It is important that the risk management process states the mechanism for identifying and reporting new risks. The whole team should be involved in this activity, and if team members are in a "risk-thinking" frame of mind then they will take advantage of opportunities to identify risks. These opportunities may occur through progress meetings, site visits, exchanges of email, quality reviews, testing, design and development activities, etc.

The nature of risks will change – some on a daily basis. The risk register needs to be able to reflect these changes. If it becomes a file that is only updated once every few weeks then it will have little value. It should be a live system. Too frequently, in my role as project auditor, I have seen dead risk registers, which are not contributing at all to the management of risk. Changes to the register may result through the performance of actions or the performance of project work. Other changes may arise from the business or marketplace. Monitoring these changes is the responsibility of the risk owners, who need to be able to suggest whether risks should be reprioritised, split out, replaced or merged with other risks. Risks are commonly split out into smaller risks if they become too difficult to manage in their present state.

There is a general view that once a risk becomes identified it stays on the risk register for a considerable time. It is, therefore, easy for risks to become stale. This can be avoided if each risk is regularly reviewed for appropriateness. If it has been too long in a particular status then action may well need to be taken. The pathway from *identification* to *actions* should be as short a duration as possible. A full register of actioned risks gives more confidence to the team than one full of risks with a status displaying *new*. Risk owners have a duty to ensure that the risks they own are regularly monitored.

From an audit point of view, an ideal situation for me is to see a risk register full of risks, an issue register with very few issues and a change control log that is equally slim. To see more issues than risks could indicate a lack of focus on risk management. I also expect to see dates that are not overdue and copious comments regarding the performance of actions.

At project close-out, there should be no risks remaining concerning the execution and delivery of the project, but there may well be risks remaining that concern the operation of the project deliverables in the business. These risks need to be transferred to the respective business owners. If a closed project was part of a programme then the programme would retain any residual risks until the programme's strategy is fulfilled. Even then, they may be some transference to a business operation.

8   Managing risk

Developing "risk-thinking" teams

In the introduction to this book I emphasised the need for team members to be thinking about risk on a daily basis. *What does this mean in practice?* I believe it means adopting a state of mind that gives overt consideration to risk whilst undertaking the various project tasks. For example, if designing a piece of user documentation, it means:

- thinking about what is being produced from the reader's point of view. *How will it be used? What is the risk of nonacceptance?*
- thinking about how the documentation links into other things being developed, such as other user documentation, training and support plans. *Who else needs to know about it? What is the risk of being out of alignment with other support objectives?*
- thinking about the length of time it will take to develop. *What is the risk of not meeting the schedule?*
- thinking about the progress to plan and not reporting a risk of noncompletion at the last minute. *What is the risk of overrun? When should any risk to the completion date be reported?*

Risk-thinking is very much about projecting into the minds of others to estimate reactions. Chess players have this ability. It is not just about thinking ahead but thinking about the consequences of future moves.

The more group sessions that can be held to identify, assess or manage risk, the better will be the buy-in to risk-thinking. Regular interaction by the team helps to dispel the view that risk management is a once-per-quarter exercise.

Creative-thinking techniques have been employed to good effect to encourage a risk-thinking approach. I have used several of these sessions, run by professional trainers, in order to generate ideas in a business process re-engineering programme. The stimulus of right-brained lateral thinking for only a short period was quite remarkable. Ideas flew thick and fast for many days following a session and the vision provided for the identification of risk was noticeably enhanced.

Certainly, I have found that the risk concept mapping technique provides a good stimulus. Not only is it highly interactive but also it is a very creative technique.

Whatever approach is taken to develop risk-thinking it is certainly worthwhile doing so. Risk-thinking does not usually come easily to project teams without a conscious effort to encourage it.

Eight things to get right

The best environment for a risk-thinking team practising good risk management is a project or programme where full attention is given to good methodology and leadership. In other words, an environment where plans are produced and maintained, progress meetings are held, changes are managed and all the elements of good project management are practised.

In my book *The Essentials of Managing Programmes* I suggest eight things to get right in a programme, all of which are traditional breeding grounds for risk. It is worthwhile repeating these eight things here as they apply equally to all the projects in a programme. There is probably no surprise as to what they are, since they represent good project management practice, so should really be present in any project methodology. It is by getting these right that risk can be significantly reduced.

Figure 8.1 shows the eight essentials and presents them as linked requirements. Because they are linked to each other it is necessary to establish all eight, in order to have a chance at achieving project and programme success.

These requirements can be important triggers for risk, some of which can be the causes of spectacular project failings. They are examined in some detail in the next few pages, and can be remembered as the mnemonic **PREPARED**:

P – Partnership; **R** – Resources; **E** – Expectations; **P** – Plans; **A** – Achievable requirements and benefits; **R** – Result; **E** – Effective sponsor; **D** – Deliverables

Lack of partnership

Many projects suffer from protracted conflicts with suppliers and third parties, arising from confusion over scope and deliverables, or misunderstandings concerning resources and timescales, for example. The prime instrument in dealing with third parties is the contract. This is usually the source of any conflict, and is the thing which needs to be right. Legally binding, it is a necessary document, but it can easily sour an otherwise good client/supplier relationship. The enthusiasm of early negotiations between a client and supplier can quickly be dimmed in protracted contractual argument. If suppliers feel the need to refer regularly to their contracts then the contracts have become a barrier to operating as a partnership.

Risk reward contracts or joint venture arrangements may be preferable to standard terms for suppliers providing the major part of services to a project. At the very least, documents of understanding should be drawn up which commit

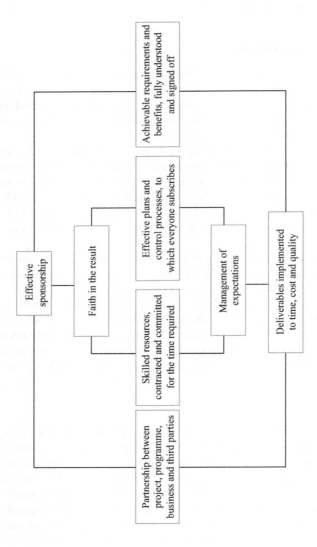

Figure 8.1 Eight things to get right

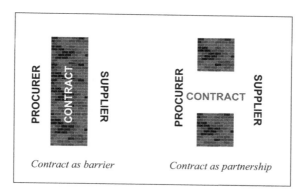

Figure 8.2 The contractual divide

suppliers to subscribing to the management processes of the project (i.e., the timely submission of progress reports, proper use of and commitment to the exceptions processes). Figure 8.2 shows the contractual divide between procurer and supplier, and suggests that a contract need not be a business barrier.

The project cannot afford to carry conflicts of management or politics, yet every large project seems to have its share of these. They are often symptomatic of the business culture and merely transferred to the project environment. The ability to work together for the greater good of the project, without conflict, is a challenging goal, and every project manager's dream, but there are techniques which can help it along. Some of these are:

* good expectations management, through regular and informed communications
* documents of understanding between project and business
* *road maps* of the project for suppliers and new starters
* plenary meetings, associated with social events
* team objectives and rewards
* proper deployment of resources
* good working conditions and environment

Poor commitment of resources

Often cited as the single, largest cause of project failure, the failure to commit resources for the time required is common in large projects, and is usually a sign of inexperienced project organisation and management.

A programme or large project may consume large numbers of resources, some of whom will be redirected from existing business operations. This is where the conflicts usually occur, and the risks of resource de-commitments are high. Much is due to poor expectation setting, and line managers can feel a lack of ownership with a project which is currently stealing the limelight.

The project manager or project director needs to establish the right priority of a project within the lines of business, and set expectations of resource requirements.

Project managers should be appointed with experience of managing project teams, and *documents of understanding* need to be drawn up (between line management and project) for all projects in order to commit resources and establish their availability without ambiguity. There must be no doubt between the lines of business and the project as to the importance and priority of committed resources' work.

Increasingly, resources are being utilised externally to projects, with work being contracted out to third parties. Resources are also contracted in, and effective use of this type of resource requires active monitoring. I have witnessed contractors whose contracts have terminated but are still performing key roles. Uncertainties or delays to contract renewal cause loss of productivity. If contractors are spending time looking for their next engagement instead of concentrating on the work in hand then they are not being managed.

The purpose of resources can easily be lost within a large project, and the Project Office needs to perform capacity planning of resources across all constituent projects to ensure their efficient and cost-effective use.

Poor or unclear expectations

Expectation setting is all about marketing, and is difficult because it is subject to changes in mood and temperament of the targeted audience. For example, in terms of engineering alone the Channel railway tunnel between England and France is a marvellous feat. However, the feat of engineering was overshadowed by the enormous financial difficulties experienced, to the extent that the positive feelings of national pride it sought to exalt were soured by the many negative feelings of a project in deep financial trouble.

There are many examples of elegant technical solutions to business problems that do not gain user acceptance because they do not meet the basic working requirement. Expectation setting is a continual process. It can be accomplished by regular user reviews of work in progress, user councils, prototyping, usability testing, etc. Whatever the method, there has to be no doubt about what is to be delivered and how it is to be used.

Ineffective plans and control processes

The managers of projects and programmes generally understand the need to establish plans and control processes, but the way in which they are utilised makes all the difference. Merely to establish processes and plans and to keep records is inadequate. They have to be effective. That is, the information they contain must be of use to the general operation of the project.

There are many examples of elegant plans being drawn up which fail to alert a project manager to signs of trouble. This is often because the plans are not analysed or planning analysis skills are not present. At the programme level, analysis is fundamental to the tracking operation. The business cannot afford to make decisions slowly, so accurate, up-to-the-minute management information is vital for steering the programme.

A common problem in projects and programmes is the lack of buy-in to standard processes by suppliers and sub-contractors. This results in the failure by third parties to submit regular progress data and to subscribe to the common planning process. Much time is wasted cajoling suppliers for vital information or converting data from inadequate software formats. This is very much a failure by the project manager in persuading suppliers to the importance of the project and their part in its success.

Requirements and benefits not achievable

Important considerations for both project requirements and benefits are:

- that it is possible to achieve them
- that business and user communities comprehend them
- that they are accepted and signed off as viable
- that a rigorous change control process exists

However, it is often requirements which cause the most friction in projects and programmes. They are more vulnerable to change, and managing requirements change is a particular challenge.

The achievability of requirements and benefits often relates to how realistic they are. "Blue sky" requirements are a venture into the unknown, often because few but the visionaries understand them. "Act-of-faith" projects are regularly commissioned, and many have been born out of the '90s vogue for globalisation. These projects stem from an ideal of global trading, cutting across country boundaries and traditions to create the truly global company. Few can say they have been totally successful, and many have cut their losses to embark on more realistic undertakings.

In the information technology sector, many projects and programmes are pioneering in nature, but enlightened organisations have learned to keep such undertakings simple and implement them step by step.

Comprehension of the requirements by all participants in a project is vital, if their translation into completed deliverables is to be effected to the correct design. Sign-offs to design documents and acceptance criteria are also vital, and the principles of change control need to be communicated to everyone involved. I have witnessed ludicrous situations where a project has reached the end of its development phase and requirements have still not been signed off by the business owners.

Lack of faith in the result

The question of faith applies equally to all those who work in a project. A determination to succeed is an important requirement not only for those at the centre of a project but also within its external suppliers. A project whose people have faith in its outcome has a definite buzz. Teams are excited about what they are accomplishing and clearly enjoy being part of it.

When teams lose faith in their ability to deliver the change as planned, morale becomes low and productivity suffers. No amount of incentive can make up for this, and the project manager needs to take regular soundings of morale across the project.

Often, loss of faith emanates from quite mundane things. I once asked a programme team member why he was dissatisfied with working on a particular programme. He replied that the journey to work every day was stressful and fraught with difficulty, and that when he arrived he was accommodated in little more than a shack! This had nothing to do with the nature of the work, which did not get a mention, but the physical environment was rated highly for job satisfaction.

Morale can vary within individual projects, and short-lived projects suffer less from poor morale than longer term projects. Work in a long-term programme can also be wearing. Some programmes have spanned several years, and 10-year programmes are not unusual, particularly in the public sector. In these situations, there needs to be variety of work and a continual sense of achievement.

Ineffective or unclear sponsorship

The Channel Tunnel, mentioned above, has presented many lessons to be learned from the people, technical and business challenges, owing to the enormous scale of the undertaking. It was not, for example, immune from ineffective or unclear sponsorship. Certainly, the UK government's insistence on private sponsorship meant that for the crucial early years of the programme there was no single backer or sponsor.

Without a single champion for a project there can be no single vision. Divided visions, from many stakeholders, often mean squabbling, awkward compromises, reduced authority and longer time for decision-making.

The role of sponsor is much misunderstood, and I have witnessed many examples of sponsors appearing in name only. Many projects aim too high in selecting their sponsors. An effective sponsor is not necessarily the chief executive, who may be far too preoccupied to become involved in a project. However, the chief executive may be the ideal choice for a company-wide programme, such as setting up global trading, since everyone in the company needs to understand that the change is being sanctioned from the very top. However, there is still work to do on the programme's behalf, even for the chief executive, so the role is more than a figurehead.

The sponsor endorses the project and acts as a sort of godfather. The sponsor might appear in publicity material endorsing the project's concepts, or the sponsor might be the first to take delivery of an end product and demonstrate that if it works for him or her then it is good for the business. More importantly, the sponsor champions the cause of the project within the context of the business as a whole. If the sponsor loses faith then the project loses its figurehead, and its direction may be far from secure.

Whilst a programme will benefit from an overall sponsor, each project needs to have its own sponsor. This should ideally be a senior management appointment in the business area concerned, in order to ensure buy-in from that business. Projects that do not have such a sponsor can suffer from a lack of commitment from their business area, which will be tested when, for example, resources are required for user testing tasks.

Deliverables not implemented to planned time, cost and quality

The trio of time, cost and quality are traditional measures of project success, but the question of whether a project is a failure if all three are not met is a question of perception. They are, however, strong contributors, and for many, extremely desirable.

Good planning and estimating will keep a grip on *time*, and good change control will ensure that "scope creep" is kept at bay. Scope creep, or the continual widening of a project scope through the piecemeal accommodation of requirements outside of change control, is also a contributor to runaway costs. Scope creep is often a contributor to the enormous differences between planned costs and actual costs in several widely reported public projects worldwide. The key question is: *Could these costs have been forecast at planning stage, and if so, would any of these projects have ever left the drawing-board?*

Quality is often a product of both cost and time, and is a particularly elusive goal. Many link the availability of increased time with the opportunity to increase quality, but attach a high cost to achieving quality. The perception of quality as high cost is, of course, false, since quality is merely the meeting of expected standards. The old adage that "the best things are achieved with time" may have some truth, but there is usually a limit to the amount of testing that any project can undertake, when a decision has to be made that the right quality standard has been reached. The classic project dilemma of *whether to increase project time to accommodate increased time for testing or to release the deliverables as completed* can only be resolved by analysis of the contributing factors. Figure 6.10 in Chapter 6, *Analysing and reporting risk*, shows how a risk analysis approach can provide suitable options for making this type of decision.

Dealing with uncertainty

In business we generally don't like uncertainty. We like to know what we are up against. So, we probe the uncertainties until we reach a point of confidence – but how far do we need to go? *As far as we need to* is the answer. As a minimum it is necessary to assess the key tasks in the project plan, asking such questions as "*Upon what are they dependent?*" and "*What is the likelihood of them being accomplished successfully?*" Examining specific areas of the project and searching for risk drivers is another essential activity, not forgetting the environment outside of the project and even outside of the company.

Each company and each project will have its own idea of the importance of risk. Even so, an appreciation of the potential showstoppers is valuable for any project. Achieving the "eight things to get right" in Figure 8.1 and understanding the risk influences in Figure 8.3 are important prerequisites. What you decide to do about them will depend on how seriously you want to manage the risk and how deeply you want to probe.

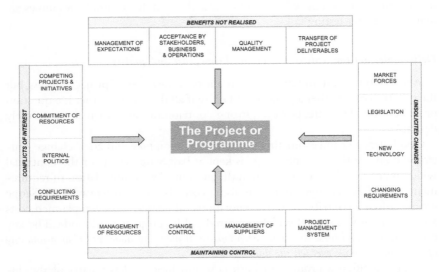

Figure 8.3 Key influences on a project or programme that need to be balanced

Take, for example, a task on the plan that requires a third party to develop a vital component, which will be integrated into a product being developed in-house. Various things could go wrong with this task:

- The component could arrive later than scheduled
- The quality of the component could be less than specified
- The wrong specification could be given to the supplier
- The component could fail an integration test into the main product
- The supplier could go into receivership

Your approach to the validity of these risks and their mitigation would depend on how critical the component was to your project and how likely you believe the risks might occur. Taking the first risk, there are any number of reasons why the component could arrive late. To what extent is it worth checking these reasons?

Let's use the benefit of hindsight and say that the risk of the component arriving late has impacted and that we are now faced with a serious issue. The reason why it was late is because an outbreak of influenza laid low all the key skills. Unlucky, you might say. Who could have foreseen that?

Well, the reason for lateness is somewhat irrelevant, since there could have been many factors causing the component to be late – the factory could have flooded, machinery could have failed, to name but two. The point is that if there is a general cause for concern that the component will be late and that each day's delay would cost a significant amount of money, then you would want to mitigate the risk of lateness and probably specify a contingency plan.

You might want to understand the combined effect of all the possible causes of risk in terms of a probability of lateness. Constructing a cause-and-effect diagram might help. Figure 8.4 shows an example, which addresses a key

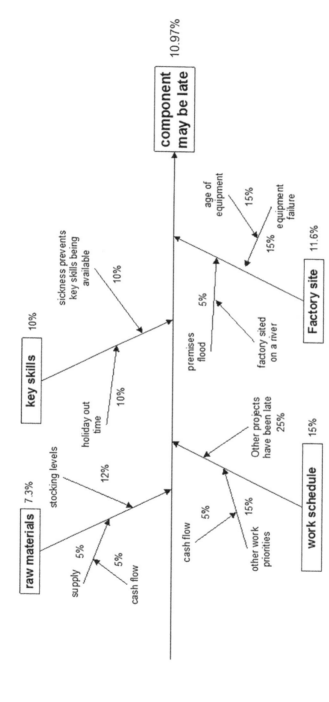

Figure 8.4 Modelling causes of lateness

concern that a supplier's component may be delivered late. The team have come together and chosen four categories that they feel could cause problems. For each category the team asks *"What could go wrong?"* and produces a top level answer. Further questioning can produce lower level answers, as required. The process requires drilling down to the underlying causes. Of course, an inspection of the supplier's site could go a long way to assessing the likelihood of many of these risks, but it is good to be prepared prior to any proposed visit. Chapter 6, *Analysing and reporting risk*, shows how this type of chart is constructed in more detail.

Often such a chart can reveal common causes. In Figure 8.3 you can see that "cash flow" appears in more than one area ("raw materials" and "work schedule"). It could also appear in "factory site" as a drill-down for "age of equipment". As described in Chapter 6, *Analysing and reporting risk*, common causes or *root causes* give a useful clue to how to tackle the risk.

The quest for certainty could be taken to extremes. The problem is that we can rarely be certain of probability and impact. Judgements have to be taken and a point of assurance has to be achieved. So, the depth of probing required, the amount of analysis and the time spent on risk management by project resources all need to be rationalised.

Risk as opportunity

In my introduction to this book I dwelt strongly on risk as a threat, but mentioned the opportunity side of risk management – the "jī" of the Chinese "wēi jī". Much time is usually spent on a project thinking of things that can go wrong. From adversity, however, springs opportunity and the use of output from a Risk Identification Workshop or a worst-case scenario map, for example, can act as a starter for examining the positive side of risk.

The best time to look for opportunities is when a set of risks has been identified and assessed. The resultant risk exposure will be good input for a debate about how to avoid carrying the amount of risk currently shown for the project. During the process of assigning actions, the question of risk avoidance should be uppermost in in the discussion, ahead of risk mitigation. The main questions to ask, of course, are: "Why are we carrying this risk? Is there not a better way?"

Risk avoidance is as much a skill as risk taking. It is also often a difficult aspect for a project team to handle. They may not feel they have the power or responsibility to make decisions about risk avoidance. They can, however, make recommendations, and these can be put to a sponsor or steering group for consideration. Small wonder then that the main activity of risk management at a team level is mainly to do with the negative aspects of risk.

Getting a sponsor involved in risk management is a key requirement. We have discussed the role of risk owner in the process, but sponsors are just as important, especially in the area of opportunity recognition. See *Risk roles* in Chapter 7, *Administering risk*, for more information on the risk role of a sponsor.

Few project teams are allocated risk KPIs,[1] where the identification of opportunities may be used to offset money deducted for threats. This requires a fairly mature approach to risk in an organisation, but can have a significant effect on business behaviours. A target risk exposure is allocated at project outset, plus or minus an amount of tolerance (see *Project start-up* in Chapter 1, *Introduction*). The control of such a KPI is through the risk assessment log, where the risk exposure is calculated after both threat and opportunity figures are multiplied together. (See *Calculating EMV* in Chapter 3, *Assessing risk*.) The effect on behaviours is to steer the team to think about avoidance, particularly when the project is carrying a large amount of threats. The risk maturity chart in Figure 8.3 shows that I rate such practice as Level 5.

Transferring risk to another party is a form of opportunity, and often answers the question "Why are we carrying this risk?" Transference can be either partial or the complete outsourcing of a piece of work or function. There can be huge cost savings, though transference is rarely total. A residual risk often remains. There also needs to be built-in control and questions such as "Will the third party perform as expected?" need to be asked through careful monitoring. For the project, it depends on whether the transference is just for the life of the project or something that has to be accommodated in the normal organisation's business operation. Again, it is usually a sponsor or senior executive who can make transference decisions.

These opportunities occur quite late in the risk management process. It is possible, though, to recognise opportunities earlier, such as in risk identification. When constructing Ishikawa diagrams to look for risk causes (see Chapter 6, *Analysing and reporting risk*), it is possible to think about the opportunities to circumvent the threats arising from the causes. Analysis of causes is not usually given much attention in project risk management, I find. Yet the causes are the seeds of possible threats or opportunities against the project. In a long-running project changes in the marketplace or business can have a significant effect on the direction of the project. Under a programme umbrella these changes are less serious as the programme is designed for change. For a stand-alone project a scope or directional change can be fatal. If a project has to close because of different business opportunities opening up, for example, that is a decision that is hopefully good for the business. Again, a sponsor with one eye on the business and one on a project is the person best placed to look out for this type of opportunity.

Much can be learned from the real risk takers, i.e., those market traders who risk their money, not for loss but for gain. Yes, they can lose money, but their constant risk-thinking approach, coupled with good data and experience, is what keeps them in their business. There is no reason why project teams should not become better at risk management over time. A company or organisation that has a roadmap to progress along the risk maturity scale should reap the rewards of good risk management sponsorship.

Avoidance strategies

Looking at the risks in Table 2.1 of Chapter 2, *Identifying and expressing risk*, what would you say are the possibilities of avoiding these risks, if any?

The key is in the causes. The first risk deals with the unavailability of board members. If it is just a question of bringing them together on a specific date, then the risk disappears. The risk does not indicate whether they would be able to sign off the requirements even if they all met to do so. This could be another risk, or at least be part of the second risk. There is no escaping the need to sign off requirements, but the opportunity is to ensure that only those who really need to sign them off do so and that any objections are known in advance and can be accommodated. The actual meeting then becomes a formality.

The second risk is a strange one in its cause but not uncommon. It is to do with perception. If there is uncertainty about the scope of the project then the risk will be very relevant. The mitigation is to have stakeholders be very clear on the project's scope and objectives before work commences. Apart from sending the entire business on a decision-making course, the cause is something that has to be accepted by the project. The opportunity is to save considerable money on change control by preventing scope changes during the key design and development phases.

The third risk relates to a particular cause, which needs careful investigation. The opportunity is to negotiate with the client to confirm his intention to proceed and so save unnecessary project work. The requirements in this case are usually contractual, so work should not proceed without their sign-off.

The fourth risk is similar. Is it credit control by the client? Again, the underlying reason needs to be investigated. The risk is almost an issue, since the current budgetary period may not have much further to run. The opportunity is to make an accounting accrual whilst urgent discussions take place with the client.

This exercise reveals how specific the causes need to be in order to take appropriate avoidance actions. Opportunity recognition needs good data and a commitment to spend time on it. Risk KPIs can focus attention on this, of course.

Avoidance strategies are often concerned with finding different ways to do things. The analysis in Figure 8.4 could result in finding a different supplier. For other risks, outsourcing a piece of work is another avoidance strategy that can be taken. Checking for unnecessary work and removing a piece of work altogether is another form of avoidance. Partial avoidance may be possible for certain risks. For example, the probability of the risk occurring might be avoided or its impact. It is often easier, though, to mitigate risk than to avoid it, so particular time and effort needs to be spent in seeing whether avoidance can be taken.

Note

1 Key performance indicators

9 Conclusion

I hope this basic survey of risk management has enabled you to understand how you can confidently employ a good risk management process for your projects and programmes. Hopefully, the techniques examined in this book will allow you to select the most appropriate level of granularity for your projects and programmes. I also hope that they will show that risks can be expressed, quantified and managed, and that risk management is not a black art but something that can be practised by all.

There is much more that I could have written, but I feel it important not to produce a weighty volume. Rather I have chosen to concentrate on what I consider to be the essential elements of good risk management, providing a few practical tools for the management of risk that I have used in tough practice.

The key messages I've tried to convey are:

1. Risk management is not a mysterious or secretive activity. It can be as practical as project planning once you know how to do it.
2. Risk management is not a negative concept. It can be used positively to improve margins and productivity. Significant opportunities can arise through its practice.
3. Everyone in the project team can practise risk management, including customers, suppliers, sponsors and business operations.
4. Risk management is a daily concern, not a once-per-quarter consideration.
5. Risk management is not a stand-alone activity. It should be part of all the project processes: reporting, scheduling, issue management, change control, cost management and quality control, to name but a few.
6. The risk-issue-change pathway is real. Major expense and time can be saved through focussing on risks before they become issues and before they become costly changes.

I wish your projects and programmes success, hoping that from now on risk management will be a major feature in them all.

Appendix A

Sample risk management procedure

NB. This procedure is an example for a project using a paper-based system. You may adopt it or adapt it for your own organisation. Please acknowledge the source.

Objective

The objective of the risk management process is to ensure that all project risks (see *Definition* section) are clearly identified and managed to a successful conclusion. Many project issues emanate from risks that could have been foreseen, but risks can only be identified if a firm risk management process is in place, to which all team members are committed. Dealing with a risk is usually much cheaper than having to deal with an issue, and even cheaper than having to make a project change. It also avoids the sudden *fire-fighting* which often has to be undertaken to tackle it when it impacts.

Scope

The risk management process covers the action to be taken at all management levels of the project and includes:

- the identification of a risk according to defined criteria (see *Definition* section)
- the assessment of each risk by relevant project personnel in terms of probability and consequence of impact
- the appointment of a Risk Owner to be responsible for ensuring that each risk is contained
- the appointment of Action Owners to carry out assigned actions to reduce, avoid or mitigate each risk
- the maintenance of a risk register and log
- the periodic review of all outstanding risks
- the analysis of key risks
- the running of regular risk assessment and risk management workshops, in order to promote concerted input to the risk process

Definition

"*A risk is a potential occurrence which may impact the outcome of the project*". **Risk management** is the process that deals with risk and contains the following four steps:

1. **Risk identification**
   - the identification, evaluation and prioritisation of risk
2. **Risk assessment**
   - the qualitative and quantitative assessment of risk (likelihood of outcomes and costing of impacts)
3. **Risk planning**
   - the assignment of containment and contingency actions
4. **Risk control**
   - the analysis of risks, regular maintenance of risk action plans, risk reassessment, risk resolution; the identification of new risks; risk reporting and review

Risk process

The risk process is shown in Table A.1 below.

Table A.1 Risk process flow diagram

Any team member identifies a risk by completing a Risk Control Form		
↓		
Team member's Sub-Project Manager validates risk, and, if valid, forwards it to the Project Office	→ Project Office logs it in the system and reviews immediately with Project Manager if risk is urgent	**NEW**
↓		
Project Manager assigns a Risk Owner	→ Project Office updates log	**ASSIGNED**
↓		
Risk Owner evaluates risk with Sub-Project Manager and/or Project Manager	→ Project Office updates log	**ASSESSED**
↓		
Risk Owner ensures containment actions are added and Action Owners are appointed	→ Project Office updates log	**ACTIONED**
↓		
Action Owners agree action plans with Risk Owner, Project Manager and Sub-Project Manager, as appropriate		
↓		
Action Owners carry out actions		
↓		
Risks and effect of actions are reviewed at Weekly Progress Meetings	→ Project Office updates log	

Actions and responsibilities

Any team member

1. Any team member may identify a situation believed to be a risk and raise a *Risk Control Form*, forwarding it to the Project Office. The risk should first be discussed with the team member's Sub-Project Manager, in order to validate the risk and provide more information regarding likelihood of occurrence and severity of impact.

Project Manager

1. The Project Manager receives Risk Control Forms from the Project Office and will assign a person to act as *Risk Owner*. This may be someone in a work area directly affected by the risk or perhaps someone suitably qualified technically with the nature of the risk.
2. The Project Manager will assign the appropriate classification level (see *Classification* section).
3. The Project Manager may decide to call a special meeting to evaluate the risk or to delegate suitably qualified personnel to evaluate it.
4. The Project Manager will review the status of each risk notification at project progress meetings.
5. The Project Manager will escalate significant risks to the steering group and/or sponsor for resolution.
6. The Project Manager will track the status of all risks, ensuring that evaluations are received and actions progressed.
7. The Project Manager is responsible for ensuring that the team actively identifies project risks and is accountable for the successful containment of all risks identified.

Project Office

1. The Project Office receives and logs Risk Control Forms into the risk management system and passes them to the Project Manager for evaluation. The Project Office will send copies of the Risk Control Form to relevant Sub-Project Managers for evaluation.
2. The original form and attachments are filed in the Project Control Book.
3. The Project Office updates the log at each stage of the risk management process, recording the actions assigned to contain the risk.

Risk Owner

•   The Risk Owner identifies *Action Owners,* who are the most appropriate persons to manage the actions to contain the risk.

Action Owners

•   The Action Owners execute actions to contain, reduce or avoid the risk.

Sub-Project Manager

- The Sub-Project Manager will assess the impact of the proposed risk upon the sub-project, noting any dependent interfaces to other sub-projects.

Steering Group

- The Steering Group will debate and attempt to contain risks, as required. They will also give approvals where necessary for contingency plans and the release of appropriate funds.

Authorities

Raising risks: Any project member
Accepting risks as valid: Sub-Project Managers
Assessing impact of risks: Sub-Project Managers, Risk Owner and Project Manager

Prioritisation

Risks will be prioritised on a severity basis (a combination of probability and impact), as follows:

3: A risk with a LOW probability and LOW to MEDIUM impact.
2: A risk with a MEDIUM probability and MEDIUM to HIGH impact.
1: A risk with a HIGH probability and HIGH to VERY HIGH impact.

Actions will be prioritised as follows:

1. An action that must be undertaken urgently
2. An action that should be undertaken within two to four weeks
3. A nonurgent action

Status codes

Risks

NEW: The Risk Control Form has been received and the risk is being dealt with.
ASSIGNED: A Risk Owner has been assigned.
ASSESSED: The risk has been assessed in terms of probability and impact.
ACTIONED: Actions have been assigned to reduce, avoid or contain the risk.
CLOSED: The risk is no longer a threat.
IMPACTED: The risk has impacted and has been converted to an issue.

Actions

NEW: An action has been specified.
ASSIGNED: An Action Owner has been assigned.

ASSESSED: The risk has been assessed as valid by the Project Manager.
IN PROGRESS: The action is being carried out.
COMPLETED: The action has been carried out.

The Risk Control Form

Each risk is recorded on a Risk Control Form. A collection of Risk Control Forms represents the *risk register* for the project and will be held centrally within the Project Office. Team members need complete only fields 2–5, 7–9 and 13, attaching supporting documentation as appropriate. Team members may also complete fields 10, 15, 16 and 17, though these may be done later by the Project Manager, in consultation with the Risk Owner and originator of the risk or through formal assessment sessions. The Project Office should complete the *Response* fields in conjunction with the Action Owners and Risk Owners.

The form is in three parts, representing three distinct phases of risk assessment: *Identification, Assessment* and *Response*. The form is not designed to be completed all at once. It is important to have a risk recorded as soon as it is known, so only basic identification fields need to be completed initially.

Identification

1. **Risk No.**:
   - a unique reference number, completed by the Project Office, e.g., R1611001, meaning R (risk), 16 (year 2016), 11 (month), 001 (numerical sequence within the month). This enables the age of outstanding risks to be easily identified.
2. **Sub-project**:
3. **Area affected**:
4. **Raised by**:
   - the originator of the risk
5. **Date raised:**
6. **Risk status:**
   - status code from section above (completed by the Project Office)
7. **Cause:**
   - enter the cause in the format "because of . . ."
8. **Risk:**
   - enter the risk in the format "risk of/that . . .". Do not describe the risk in great detail. Attach any detailed explanation as supporting documentation, as required.
9. **Impact:**
   - enter the impact in the format "resulting in . . ."

Assessment

10. Prob. %

- enter the percentage chance of the probability of the risk occurring (0%–99%)

11. Impact %:

- an assessment of the impact to the project budget in % (completed by the Project Manager)

12. Risk Owner:

- the name of the Risk Owner (completed by the Project Manager)

13. Time window:

- an estimate in months of when the risk might impact

14. Priority:

- the severity code, as described in *Prioritisation* section earlier

15. RE £K:

- enter the risk exposure in £K (Probability % x Impact Cost £K)

16. Impact Cost £K:

- estimate the cost of impact in £K

17. Evaluation criteria:

- a brief description of why the risk was assessed as it was in 15 and 16 above

Response

18. Action No.:

- a unique reference number, completed by the Project Office, e.g., A1611001, meaning A (action), 16 (year 2016), 11 (month), 001 (numerical sequence within the month). This enables the age of outstanding actions to be easily identified.

19. Response action:

- list each action to contain the risk

20. Action Owner:

- the person(s) responsible for carrying out the action

21. Priority:

- the action code, as described in *Prioritisation* section earlier

22. Due Date:

- the date the action must be completed

23. Reduction Prob. %:

- the percentage reduction in probability if the action is successful

24. Reduction Impact %:

- the percentage reduction in impact to the project budget if the action is successful

25. Action Cost £K:

- the estimated cost of the action in £K

26. Action status:

- the status of the action described above, plus date and comments for codes 2 to 5 (completed by the Project Office on behalf of Action Owners)

Meetings and reports

The status of risks will be discussed at summary level during weekly project progress meetings. The Project Manager will use the risk log to review risks at the meeting, having first checked the status of each risk with the Risk Owners.

Separate Risk Reviews may be called by the Project Manager as required to discuss the nature of risks, their impact and cost of resolution. The Project Manager will also give a summary status of risks at steering group meetings.

The Project Manager may, from time to time, run group risk identification and assessment sessions, which focus on the whole project or on a specific part.

Risk analysis

The Project Manager, in consultation with the Risk Owner and originator, will assess the probability of the risk occurring and its impact. These may change during the life of the risk, as actions are completed to reduce its likelihood or impact or new information becomes available.

Appendix B
Sample risk register

NB. You may adopt this sample or adapt it for your own organisation. Please acknowledge the source.

Table B.1 Sample risk register

Risk No.	Sub-Project	Area Affected	Raised By	Date Raised	Risk Status

Cause	Risk	Impact
Because of	there is a risk that	resulting in

Prob. %	Impact %	Risk Owner	Time Window	Priority	Risk Exposure £K	Impact Cost £K	Assessment comments

Action No.	Response Action	Action Owner	Priority	Due Date	Reduction in Prob.%	Reduction in Impact %	Cost £K	Action Status

Bibliography

APM (2004) *Project Risk Analysis and Management Guide (PRAM)*, 2nd edition. High Wycombe: APM Publishing. ISBN 1-903494-12-5.

Bartlett, John (1992) *Managing Business Risks in Major IT Projects*. High Wycombe: APM Journal Project.

Bartlett, John (1994) *Invest in a Firm Foundation to Manage Risk Throughout a Project*. Proceedings of 12th IPMA World Congress on Project Management, Oslo.

Bartlett, John (1998, 2000, 2002, 2005, 2006) *Managing Programmes of Business Change*, 4th edition. London: Project Manager Today Publications. ISBN 1-900391-08-2.

Bartlett, John (2005) *Right First and Every Time – Managing Quality in Projects and Programmes*. London: Project Manager Today Publications. ISBN 1-900391-13-9.

Bartlett, John (2016) *The Essentials of Managing Programmes*. Abingdon: Routledge.

Bartlett, John (2017) *The Essentials of Managing Quality for Projects and Programmes*. Abingdon: Routledge.

Bartlett, John (2017) *The Essentials of Managing Risks for Projects and Programmes*. Abingdon: Routledge.

CCTA (1995) *Management of Programme Risk* (John Bartlett for CCTA). London: HMSO. ISBN 0-11-330672-5.

Checkland, Peter (1981) *Systems Thinking, Systems Practice*. Chichester: John Wiley.

Hillson, David (September 2000) Project Risks – Identifying Causes, Risks and Effects. *PM Network*, Project Management Institute, Vol. 14, No. 9, pages 48–51.

Hillson, David (2004) *Effective Opportunity Management for Projects: Exploiting Positive Risk*. New York: Marcel Dekker. ISBN 0-8247-4808-5.

Hillson, David and Murray-Webster, Ruth (2007) *Understanding and Managing Risk Attitude*, 2nd edition. Aldershot, UK: Gower. ISBN 978-0-566-08798-1.

Hillson, David and Murray-Webster, Ruth (2008) *Managing Group Risk Attitude*. Aldershot, UK: Gower. ISBN 978-0-566-08787-5.

Institution of Civil Engineers and the Faculty and Institute of Actuaries (1998) *RAMP Risk Analysis and Management for Projects*. London: Thomas Telford Ltd. ISBN 0-7277-2697-8.

OGC (2002, 2004, 2007, 2010) *Management of Risk (MOR): Guidance for Practitioners*. London: TSO. ISBN 978-0-113-31274-0.

Watson, Richard and Ramsay, Cameron (2000) *Focussing Project Risk Management to Enhance Business Performance*. 4th Annual Risk Symposium, London, 11 October 2000 (later republished in two parts in *Project Manager Today*, April and May 2001).

Wilson, Brian (2000) *Systems: Concepts, Methodologies and Applications*. Chichester: John Wiley & Sons Ltd. ISBN 0-471-92716-3.

Wilson, Brian (2001) *Soft Systems Methodology – Concept Model Building and Its Contribution.* Chichester: John Wiley & Sons Ltd.

Suggestions for further study

In the UK, the Association for Project Management (website: www.apm.org) is a valuable source of information for risk management in a project and programme context. Its Risk Management Specific Interest Group meets to debate current techniques and experiences in the subject, and articles appear regularly in its journal *Project*. Similarly, the US-based Project Management Institute (PMI) (website: www.pmi.org) also features papers and articles on risk management and has sub-groups (known as chapters) around the world.

The independent magazine *Project Manager Today* features regular risk management articles, and risk management is often a focus for its well-known seminars and conferences (website: www.pmtoday.co.uk).

The UK Institute of Risk Management (website: www.theirm.org) is a professional body dedicated to risk management, providing a forum for the subject, together with certification.

Glossary

Term	Meaning	Chapters
Action owner	Someone who owns an action to address a risk.	4, 5, 7
Business	Often used as a generic term for a company's business operation.	2
Business case	Business and financial justification for a programme or project.	1
Business Change Manager	A role in a programme that monitors strategy.	2
Business strategy	A statement of business direction and goals.	2
Cause-and-effect diagram	A fish-bone type diagram showing contributing causes to a single outcome.	6, 8
Change	An alteration to a project or programme that is exceptional to the current specification, requirements, management, goals or timescale.	2
Change control	The logging and control of changes in a project or programme.	2
Contingency	An alternative action plan in case a risk impacts, thus avoiding the impact, or an amount of money set aside in case of risk impact.	1, 3, 4
Decision tree	A chart of events and decisions designed to aid the choice of suitable options.	6
Exception	An exceptional event (risk, issue or change) in a project or programme.	1

Term	Meaning	Chapters
Focus area	Sections of a project or business that can be selected for particular attention, to aid in risk identification, for example.	2, 6
Impact	The result of a risk occurring.	3
Influence diagram	A flow diagram showing decisions in relation to chance events.	6
Ishikawa diagram	Another name for *Cause-and-effect diagram*.	6
Issue	An immediate problem requiring resolution.	2
Mitigation	A type of risk response action that lessens severity (i.e., impact and/or probability).	4
Monte Carlo simulation	A form of risk modelling to show a range of possible outcomes for dates or costs.	6
Probability	The likelihood of a risk occurring.	3
Probability/Impact Matrix	A chart showing probability against impact.	6
Programme	A collection of vehicles for change designed to achieve a strategic objective.	1
Project	A vehicle for change that is transient and has a defined start and end date.	1
Radar Chart	A type of chart to show the extent of risk in different focus areas.	6
Ribbon Chart	A type of chart to show the extent of risk in three dimensions.	6
Risk	A potential future event that could affect a project or programme.	2
Risk analysis	The use of risk data to enable decisions to be made concerning risk in a project.	6
Risk assessment	The estimation and evaluation of risk for qualification and/or quantification, usually in terms of priority, probability and cost of impact.	3
Risk Assessment Workshop	A form of workshop designed to enable participants to assess risks and plan response actions.	3

(Continued)

Term	Meaning	Chapters
Risk avoidance	Working around a risk so that the risk can no longer impact.	4, 8
Risk checklist	A list of things to consider when identifying risk, often compiled from previous experience.	1, 2
Risk concept map	A flow diagram to show situations that could trigger risk, leading to increasing severity of impacts.	6
Risk exposure	A calculation of the cost of risk impacts to a project or programme.	3
Risk Identification Workshop	A form of workshop designed to enable participants to identify risks.	2
Risk log	A one-line summary of each risk in a risk register.	5
Risk management	An umbrella term for the identification, assessment, response, analysis and control of risk.	7
Risk management procedure	A description of the process that all project members should follow for the management of risk.	7, App. A
Risk manager	A member of a project team particularly responsible for the management of risk.	7
Risk maturity	A scale of risk management practice.	1
Risk modelling	A way of using risk data to predict results.	6
Risk owner	A person, normally from the project team, who takes ownership for the assessment and management of response actions for a risk.	2, 7
Risk planning	An activity to plan the approach to deal with evaluated risks.	1
Risk priority	The importance to the project of a risk in relation to other risks; a signal to tackle the highest priority risks first.	3
Risk register	A repository for the recording and control of risk, either paper-based or a software application.	5

Term	Meaning	Chapters
Risk reserves	Money set aside in case risks impact.	1
Risk response	A plan of actions to deal with assessed risks.	4
Risk statement	A sentence that describes the cause, risk event and impact of a risk.	2, 6
Root cause	The lowest level of common cause, often revealed in a *Cause-and-effect diagram*.	6, 8
Scope creep	The gradual widening of a project's scope through the addition of changes.	8
Severity	In risk terms, a combination of probability and impact.	2
Soft Systems Methodology	A modelling technique for human activity systems developed by Lancaster University in the 1980s.	6
Spider Chart	A type of chart to show the extent of risk in different focus areas.	6
Sponsor	A senior manager or executive responsible for acting as business champion for a project or programme.	7
Steering group	A body responsible for steering the programme.	7, 8
Tolerance	A range of financial measures by which a project manager has control.	1, 3

Index

For Product Safety Concerns and Information please contact our EU
representative GPSR@taylorandfrancis.com Taylor & Francis Verlag GmbH,
Kaufingerstraße 24, 80331 München, Germany

Printed and bound by CPI Group (UK) Ltd, Croydon, CR0 4YY

08/05/2025

01864403-0001